PROPHETS 1

Volume Three

The Last Prophet

may Allah bless him and grant him peace

Ahmad Thomson

Ta-Ha Publishers Ltd
LONDON – NEW YORK

Copyright © Ahmad Thomson   Rabia'l-Awwal 1421 / June 2000

Published by

Ta-Ha Publishers Ltd
1 Wynne Road
London SW9 0BB

website: http://taha.co.uk
email   :   sales@taha.co.uk

All rights reserved. No part of this publication may be reproduced, stored in any retrieval system, or transmitted in any form or by any means, electronic or otherwise, without written permission from the publishers, except for passages for review purposes.

Typeset by Ahmad Thomson

British Library Cataloguing in Publication Data

A catalogue record for this book is available from the British Library

ISBN 1 84200 014 4

Printed and bound in Great Britain by
Deluxe Printers, London

website: http://www.de-luxe.com
email   :   de-luxe@talk21.com

Contents

Foreword	vii
Song Written before the Prophet	xii
The Prophet Muhammad may Allah bless him and grant him peace	1
The Qualities of Muhammad	101
Glossary of Arabic Terms	105
Bibliography	121

*Allahumma salli ala sayyedina Muhammidan
abdika wa rasulika'n-nabiyyi'l-ummiyy
wa ala alihi wa sahbihi wa sallim*

O Allah, bless our master Muhammad,
Your slave and Your Messenger, the unlettered Prophet,
and his family and his companions and grant them peace.

Acknowledgements

This book is dedicated to my teacher Shaykh Abdalqadir as-Sufi ad-Darqawi al-Murabit, who was the first to tell me about the Last Prophet, Muhammad, may Allah bless him and grant him peace, and it is dedicated to whoever embraces Islam and follows in the dust of his footseps.

I would also like to acknowledge and pay tribute to the work of Hajj 'Abdalhaqq and A'i'sha Abdarrahman at-Tarjumana Bewley, whose illuminating translations from Arabic into English have made not only the Qur'an but also numerous other essential texts accessible to English speaking Muslims. Most of the translations – especially from *Al-Muwatta'* of Imam Malik, *Ash-Shifa'* of Qadi 'Iyad and the *Diwan* of Shaykh Muhammad ibn al-Habib, may Allah be pleased with them – which are quoted in the following pages are theirs.

*Allahumma salli ala sayyedina Muhammidan
abdika wa rasulika'n-nabiyyi'l-ummiyy
wa ala alihi wa sahbihi wa sallim*

O Allah, bless our master Muhammad,
Your slave and Your Messenger, the unlettered Prophet,
and his family and his companions and grant them peace.

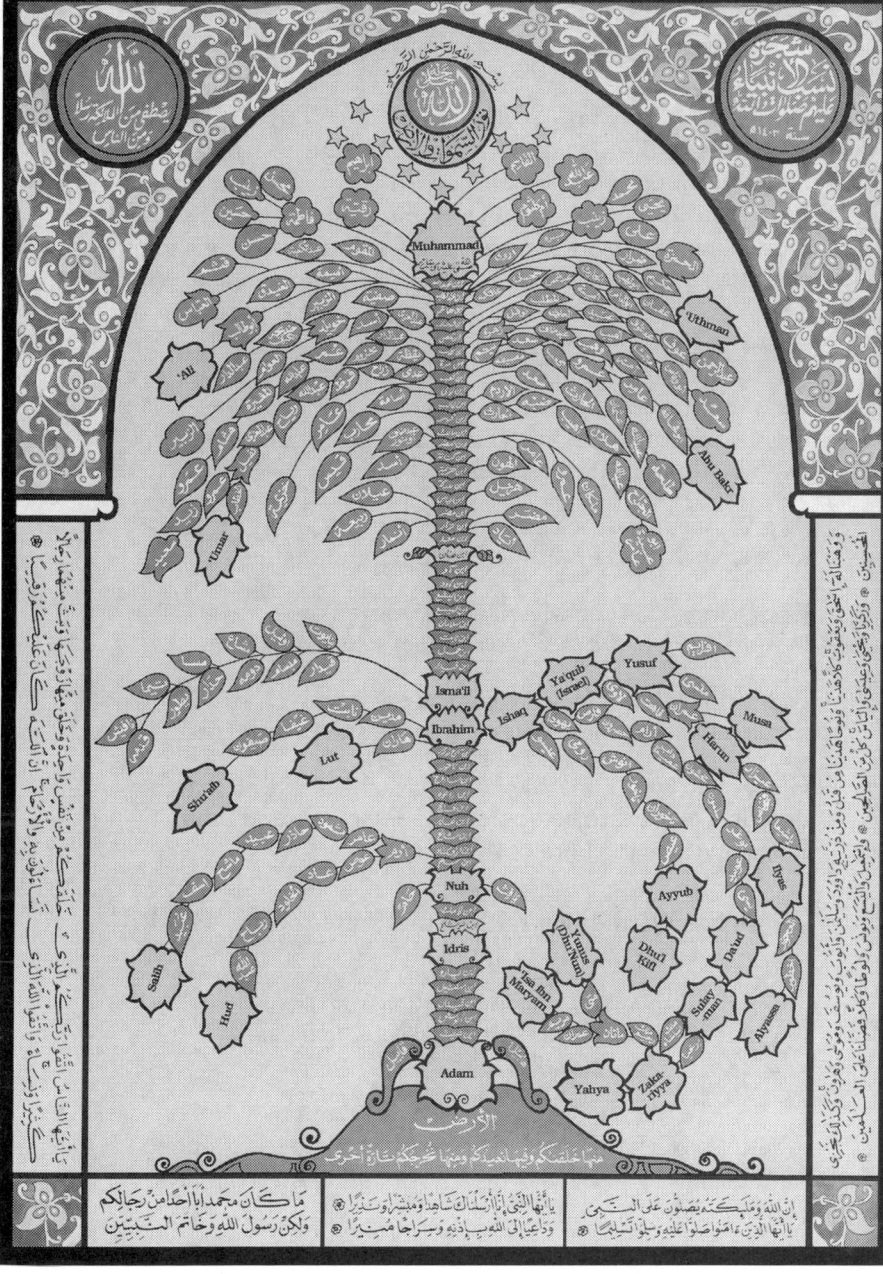

The Treasury of Truths

Oh Allah, bless and grant peace to our lord and master Muhammad, the first of the lights emanating from the oceans of the sublimity of the essence, with every one of Your perfections in all Your self-manifestations, in the two worlds – the hidden and the seen – he realises the meanings of the names and attributes. He is the first to give praise and worship with every kind of adoration and good action. He is the helper of all created beings in the world of forms and the world of spirits. And blessings be upon his family and Companions with a blessing that will lift the veil from his noble face for us in visions and in the waking state and will acquaint us with You and with him in all ranks and presences.

Be gracious to us, oh Mawlana, by his rank,
in movement and in stillness, in looks and in thoughts.

Be gracious to us, oh Mawlana, by his rank,
in movement and in stillness, in looks and in thoughts.

Be gracious to us, oh Mawlana, by his rank,
in movement and in stillness, in looks and in thoughts.

Glory be to your Lord, the Lord of Might, above all that they describe, and peace be upon the messengers, and praise belongs to Allah, the Lord of the worlds.

(From the Wird of Shaykh Muhammad ibn al-Habib)

*Allahumma salli ala sayyedina Muhammidan
abdika wa rasulika'n-nabiyyi'l-ummiyy
wa ala alihi wa sahbihi wa sallim*

O Allah, bless our master Muhammad,
Your slave and Your Messenger, the unlettered Prophet,
and his family and his companions and grant them peace.

❁   ❁   ❁   ❁   ❁

بِسْمِ اللَّهِ الرَّحْمَنِ الرَّحِيمِ

Foreword

This book, *Prophets in the Qur'an – Volume Three*, is the last in the *Prophets in the Qur'an* series. Whereas *Volumes One* and *Two* consider all the Prophets mentioned in the Qur'an from the first Prophet to appear on earth, *sayyedina* Adam, up to and including *sayyedina* 'Isa, *Volume Three* considers the last Prophet to appear on earth, *sayyedina* Muhammad, may the blessings and peace of Allah be on him, and on all the Prophets, and on all the sincere followers of all the Prophets. Everything that was stated in the Forewords to *Volumes One* and *Two* applies equally to *Volume Three* and need not be repeated again here.

So much is known about the Prophet Muhammad, may Allah bless him and grant him peace, and so much has been written about him, that it is always a daunting task to attempt to write more, even when it is in the hope that the end result will be an account which is accurate, reliable and of use to the reader – and which does not merely duplicate what has already been written by someone else. This is especially the case concerning knowledge about the Prophet Muhammad, although it applies equally to knowledge about all the other Prophets as well, may the blessings and peace of Allah be on him and them, since knowledge of the Prophets – and this includes knowledge of the knowledge which they brought – depends essentially on transmission, and not on opinion. The only real service which an author can hope to provide is to present aspects of reliably transmitted knowledge in such a way that it becomes more accessible to the reader than it otherwise might have been.

This knowledge is so vast that it is indeed an ocean without a shore, and in such an ocean it is possible to lose both direction and sense of proportion. It might therefore appear in the context of this series – *Prophets in the Qur'an*, in which emphasis has been placed on what the Qur'an itself says about the Prophets that it mentions, as opposed to what is to be found in the *hadith* or other historical sources – that the task of writing about the Prophet Muhammad would be relatively simple, since he is in fact only directly mentioned by name in the Qur'an in relatively few *ayat*.

It is clear, however, that many of the *ayat* in the Qur'an are either addressed directly to the Prophet Muhammad, may Allah bless him and grant him peace, or else they are about him – and in fact the more deeply anyone studies the Qur'an, the more he or she inevitably discovers that it is necessary to have an intimate knowledge both of the history of the Prophet Muhammad's life and of the place and time in which each *ayah* was revealed, and of what the Prophet Muhammad said about the meaning of each *ayah*, if one is really going to understand the full significance of these *ayat* and of the Qur'an as a whole.

It is for this reason that it is important for anyone who studies and wishes to follow the Qur'an to have access to the reliable *tafsirs*, or commentaries, on the Qur'an since these record transmitted knowledge about the meanings of the *ayat*, a knowledge which was transmitted to and from the best of the Prophet Muhammad's companions, from the Prophet Muhammad himself.

Even more importantly, it is necessary for anyone who studies and wishes to follow the Qur'an to have access to a *living* human being who knows and understands the Qur'an by heart, and who is familiar with and understands the *tafsirs* on the Qur'an – in other words, a person to whom this knowledge has been transmitted by his teacher, who had it from his teacher, who had it from his teacher … and so on … right back to the Companions of the Prophet Muhammad, and so to the Prophet Muhammad himself, may the blessings and peace of Allah be on him and on his family and on his companions and on all who follow him and them with sincerity in what they are able until the Last Day. Anyone who relies only on books is likely to end up being overwhelmed by a mountain of information, some of which may well have been either misinterpreted or not fully appreciated, either because there is a serious lack of basic knowledge – and accordingly of balance and understanding – or else because of the even more serious lack of human transmission. Everyone needs a teacher.

Bearing this in mind, and faced with such a vast choice of what could be written, what appears in the following pages is a very limited selection from what is actually available. This selection has been based primarily on the direct references to the Prophet Muhammad which appear in the Qur'an, may Allah bless him and grant him peace, and then on what some of the reliable commentators have said concerning these *ayat*.

Since it is essential to appreciate the unique purity of the Message as well as the unique character of the Messenger – for otherwise it would not be possible to place one's complete trust in either of them – both the qualities of the Qur'an itself as well as the qualities of the Prophet Muhammad himself, may Allah bless him and grant him peace, are considered in the pages which follow – and since the knowledge of Allah which the Prophet Muhammad was granted was both unique and unsurpassed, both the *ayat* of the Qur'an and some of the relevant *hadith* which describe what occurred on his miraculous Night Journey – from Makka to Jerusalem and then through the realms of the seven heavens beyond the limit of forms, the *sidrat al-muntaha*, to within two bows' lengths or nearer to the Presence of the Allah – are examined in detail.

As was the case when writing *Volume Two*, the renowned work of *Ash-Shifa'* of *Qadi* 'Iyad, translated into English by Hajj Abdalhaqq and 'A'isha Bewley, has proved invaluable, since *Qadi* 'Iyad, may Allah be pleased with him, possessed a vast, reliable and well-balanced knowledge and understanding both of these *ayat* and of the commentaries on them. Virtually everything in his *Ash-Shifa'* consists of what had been transmitted to him. He hardly ever ventures to express a personal opinion, other than to express a personal preference for a particular interpretation – and the reasons for having expressed that particular preference – whenever there is more than one possible interpretation.

Thus it is clear that *Qadi* 'Iyad was only concerned with conveying reliable knowledge about Allah and His Messenger – and not with trying to attract praise towards himself.

Another factor which influenced the contents of what appears in the following pages is the desire to clarify the very close connection which exists between all of the Prophets, not only as regards their knowledge of Reality – of Allah – and not only as regards their way of life – Islam – but also, in an age when this is not always realised or appreciated, their knowledge of each other.

For the Qur'an makes it clear that each Prophet was not only aware that the Prophet Muhammad would come, but also promised to support and follow him if he should come during his own particular life-time:

> And when Allah made His covenant with the Prophets, (He said), 'This is what I have given you as a Book and wisdom, and then a Messenger (Muhammad) will come to you confirming what you have – and you will believe in him and you will help him.'
>
> He said, 'Will you be bound by this and will you accept this obligation?' They replied, 'We will be bound by it.'
>
> He said, 'Then bear witness to it – and I will bear witness with you – and as for whoever turns away after this, then they will be the ones who disobey.' (3.81-82).

And:

> And (remember) when We made a covenant with the Prophets – with you (Muhammad), and with Nuh, and Ibrahim, and Musa, and 'Isa son of Maryam – and We made them make a solemn covenant, so that the truthful might be asked about their truthfulness – and He has prepared a painful punishment for the disbelievers. (33.7-8).

As we shall see in more detail in the pages that follow, this covenant which was made near the 'beginning' of time was confirmed towards the 'end' of time, when the Prophet Muhammad met many of the earlier Prophets during his miraculous Night Journey, and indeed led them in prayer, may the blessings and peace of Allah be on him and them. This close spiritual relationship between all of the Prophets will of course become even more apparent on the Last Day, when everyone who has ever lived – including all of the Prophets and their respective followers and communities – will be brought back to life by Allah to have the actions and intentions which they had in this world weighed in the balance, before being sent either to the Garden or to the Fire.

Since the Prophet Muhammad often talked about what would happen on that Day, may Allah bless him and grant him peace, some of the *ayat* and *hadith* which describe this appointment with Allah – an appointment which no one will be able to avoid – are considered, especially those concerning the Prophet Muhammad's high station with Allah on that Day, and his interceding for his community.

There has always been the danger for those who believe in Allah and His Prophets that either the Message or the Messenger will be worshipped instead of the One who sent them. In every age there have been people who either idolised a revelation or worshipped the one to whom it was originally revealed. Accordingly there is also a section in the pages which follow which is concerned with what *adab* is acceptable – as well as what is necessary – towards the Prophet Muhammad, not only inwardly, but also outwardly, and especially whenever a follower of the Prophet Muhammad visits him at his graveside in Madina, may Allah bless him and grant him peace.

Part of what each Prophet covenanted with Allah to do was to deliver the message with which he had been entrusted by Allah, to his people. Thus when the Prophet Muhammad was approaching the end of his life on earth, may Allah bless him and grant him peace, and when he gave his famous *khutba* on the farewell pilgrimage, he asked the people who were present, 'Have I delivered the message?' – and they all replied, 'Yes!'

Thus it should always be remembered that whatever is written about the Prophet Muhammad, may Allah bless him and grant him peace, is only ever any good if it assists in helping to convey the message which he originally delivered, and it should always be remembered that the essential purpose of that message was to show people how to worship Allah, not blindly but with knowledge and understanding – for that is the meaning of man:

I did not create the *jinn* and mankind except to worship Me.

(51.56).

And were it not for the means, the end would have escaped us:

Say (O Muhammad): 'If you love Allah, then follow me, and Allah will love you and forgive you your wrong actions,' – and Allah is Forgiving, Compassionate. (3.31).

It has been related by at-Tirmidhi that the Messenger of Allah, may Allah bless him and grant him peace, said to Anas ibn Malik, 'Whoever gives life to my *sunna* has loved me and whoever loves me is with me in the Garden.' May Allah put that love in your heart.

Ahmad Thomson
London, 1421 / 2000

Song Written before the Prophet

We are present in the garden of the Prophet,
seeking acceptance and welcome.
We have come, O best of refuges,
bowed in humility and bewilderment.

Ask Allah to give us every help,
that we may attain our desire at the time debts fall due.
You have a vast power which is beyond compare
and a message greater than every messenger's.
You are the door to Allah in every good thing –
whoever comes to you gains acceptance and union.
Every secret which came to the prophets
is from your sublimity, confirmed through transmission.

I have looked to the Prophet to plead with Allah
in my affairs, for he is the accepted intercessor.
All whose journey ends at the house of a generous host,
get what they ask for, even their most extreme desires.

We have given thanks to Allah for every time
that He has given us the gift of a visit to the Messenger
– And a visit to all those in Baqi' of the Companions
and the offspring of Fatima –
And a visit to every wife and daughter and son
of the deliverer of mankind on the day debts fall due.
And a visit to every martyr in Uhud,
and the uncle of the Messenger.

We have asked by them perfect peace for us
on our journey to our land and when we enter it.
We have sought deliverance on the Day of Gathering
and safety from the ignorant.

Our Lord, bless the Prophet and his family
and Companions and the followers.

(From the Diwan of Shaykh Muhammad ibn al-Habib)

THE PROPHET MUHAMMAD
may Allah bless him and grant him peace

Whereas virtually all the major Prophets after *sayyedina* Ibrahim were descended from his son *sayyedina* Ishaq, *sayyedina* Muhammad was descended from his son *sayyedina* Isma'il, may the blessings and peace of Allah be on them. While *sayyedina* Ibrahim and *sayyedina* Isma'il were building the Ka'aba, *sayyedina* Ibrahim made this prayer for his descendants:

> And when Ibrahim and Isma'il were raising the foundations of the House, (Ibrahim) prayed, 'Our Lord, accept this from us – surely only You are the Hearer, the Knower.
>
> 'Our Lord, and make us Muslim to You, and from our offspring a nation which is Muslim to You, and show us our ways of worship, and turn to us – surely only You are the One Who Turns in Mercy, the Compassionate.
>
> 'Our Lord, and raise up in their midst a Messenger from among them who will recite Your signs to them, and give them knowledge of the Book and the Wisdom, and make them pure – surely only You are the Mighty, the Wise.'
>
> And who leaves the way of Ibrahim except the one who fools himself? And certainly We chose him in this world, and surely in the next world he is among the righteous. When his Lord said to him, 'Submit!' he said, 'I have submitted to the Lord of the worlds.'
>
> And this is what Ibrahim commanded his sons – and also Ya'qub – (saying), 'O my sons, surely Allah has chosen the *deen* (of Islam) for you – so do not die except as Muslims.
>
> (2.127-132).

It is clear from the above passage and from other *ayat* in the Qur'an not only that the message of *all* the Messengers has always been fundamentally the same, and that their *deen* has always been fundamentally the same, but also that the Messenger to whom *sayyedina*

Ibrahim was referring in his prayer – and accordingly the answer to it – was *sayyedina* Muhammad, may Allah bless him and grant him peace:

> Now there has come to you a Messenger from among yourselves – grievous to him is your suffering, anxious is he over you, gentle to the trusting, compassionate – so if they turn their backs, say, 'Allah is enough for me, there is no god but Him – in Him I have put my trust – and He is the Lord of the Mighty Throne. (9.128-129).

And:

> Allah has indeed been gracious to the believers by raising up in their midst a Messenger from among them who recites His signs to them, and makes them pure, and gives them knowledge of the Book and the Wisdom – when before they were certainly clearly astray. (3.164).

And, in the *ayat* which commanded the Prophet Muhammad, may Allah bless him and grant him peace, to change the direction in which the Muslims face when doing the prayer, from Jerusalem to Makka:

> And from wherever you may come, (when you pray) turn your face towards the Sacred Mosque (in Makka) – and wherever you may be, turn your faces towards it, so that people have no argument against you, except those of them who do wrong – and do not be afraid of them, but fear Me – so that I may complete my blessing on you and so that you may be guided, now that We have sent a Messenger from among you to you, who recites Our signs to you, and who makes you pure, and who gives you knowledge of the Book and the Wisdom, and who teaches you what you did not know – so remember Me and I will remember you, and be grateful to Me and do not reject Me. (2.150-152).

Thus, as we have already seen:

> Ibrahim was not a Jew, and he was not a Christian, but he was *hanif* – a Muslim – and he was not one of those who worship idols.

> Surely the people who are closest to Ibrahim are those who followed him, and this Prophet (Muhammad), and those who believe – and Allah is the Friend of the believers. (3.67-68).

The Qur'an commands the believers to pray for blessings on *sayyedina* Muhammad, may Allah bless him and grant him peace:

> Surely Allah and His angels shower blessings on the Prophet – O you who believe ask for blessings on him and greet him with greetings of peace. (33.56).

It has been transmitted by Abu Mas'ud al-Ansari that Bashir ibn Sa'd said to the Prophet Muhammad, may Allah bless him and grant him peace, at the gathering of Sa'd ibn 'Ubada, 'Allah has ordered us to ask for blessings on you, Messenger of Allah. How should we do it?' Abu Mas'ud al-Ansari said, 'The Messenger of Allah, may Allah bless him and grant him peace, remained silent until we wished we had not asked him. Then he told us to say, "O Allah, bless Muhammad and the family of Muhammad as You blessed Ibrahim, and give *baraka* to Muhammad and the family of Muhammad as You gave *baraka* to the family of Ibrahim. In all the worlds You are worthy of Praise and Glorious." – "*Allahumma salli 'ala Muhammad wa ali Muhammad kama sallaita Ibrahim, wa baraka 'ala Muhammad wa ali Muhammad kama barakta 'ala ali Ibrahim. Fi'l 'alamin, innaka Hamidu'm-Majid.*"' (*Al-Muwatta'* of *Imam* Malik: 9.22.70).

This prayer not only confirms the close connection between *sayyedina* Muhammad and *sayyedina* Ibrahim, may Allah bless them and grant them peace, but also the close connection between all the believing Muslims and *sayyedina* Muhammad and *sayyedina* Ibrahim, since every one of them says this prayer – or one of the variations of it – at least five times a day, whenever they do the obligatory prayer, as well as whenever they do any voluntary prayer.

In fact, as we have already seen, it was not only *sayyedina* Ibrahim who was aware of the coming of *sayyedina* Muhammad, but indeed all the Prophets, may Allah bless them and grant them peace:

> And when Allah made His covenant with the Prophets, (He said), 'This is what I have given you as a Book and wisdom, and then a Messenger (Muhammad) will come to

you confirming what you have – and you will believe in him and you will help him.'

He said, 'Will you be bound by this and will you accept this obligation?'

They replied, 'We will be bound by it.'

He said, 'Then bear witness to it – and I will bear witness with you – and as for whoever turns away after this, then they will be the ones who disobey.' (3.81-82).

When commenting on the above passage *Qadi* 'Iyad states:

> Abu'l-Hasan al-Qabisi said about this, 'Allah singled out Muhammad for an excellence which He did not give to anyone else. He clearly states this in this *ayah*.'
>
> The commentators say that Allah made this pact by means of revelation. He did not send any Prophet without mentioning and describing Muhammad to him. The pact stipulated that if he met him, he must believe in him. It is said that the pact entailed them telling their people about him and that it stipulated that they must explain this and describe him to those coming after them. Allah's words, **'then a Messenger will come to you,'** (3.81) is in fact addressed to the People of the Book contemporary with Muhammad.
>
> 'Ali ibn Abi Talib said, 'Allah did not send any Prophet from the time of Adam onwards without making a pact with him about Muhammad. If Muhammad were sent while that Prophet was still alive, then he would have to believe in him and help him. He had to make a contract to that effect against his own people.' (*Ash-Shifa'* of *Qadi* 'Iyad: 1.1.7).

This covenant which Allah made with all of the Prophets is also mentioned in Surat al-Ahzab:

> **And (remember) when We made a covenant with the Prophets – with you, and with Nuh, and Ibrahim, and Musa, and 'Isa son of Maryam – and We made them make a solemn covenant, so that the truthful might be asked about their truthfulness – and He has prepared a painful punishment for the disbelievers. (33.7-8).**

When referring to the above *ayah*, *Qadi* 'Iyad states:

It is related that while 'Umar ibn al-Khattab was lamenting the death of the Prophet, he said, 'My father and mother be your ransom, O Messenger of Allah! It has come down that part of your excellence with Allah is that He sent you as the last of the Prophets while mentioning you among the first of them: **"When We made a pact with the Prophets, with you and with Nuh ..."** (33.7). My mother and father be your ransom, O Messenger of Allah! It has come down that part of your excellence with Him is that the people of the Fire will wish they had obeyed you even while they are being punished in its depths. They will say, **"O would that we had obeyed Allah and the Messenger!"'** (33.66).

Qatada said that the Prophet said, 'I was the first of the Prophets to be created and the last of them to be sent.' That is why he was mentioned before Nuh and the others.

As-Samarqandi said, 'Our Prophet is singled out by being mentioned before them even though he was the last of them to be sent. It means that Allah made a pact with them when He brought them out from the back of Adam like small ants.' (*Ash-Shifa'* of *Qadi* 'Iyad: 1.1.7).

Qadi 'Iyad also states:

Ibn 'Abbas said that the spirit of the Prophet was a light in the hands of Allah two thousand years before He created Adam. That light glorified Him and the angels glorified by his glorification. When Allah created Adam, He cast that light into his loins.

The Messenger of Allah said, 'Allah brought me down to earth in the loins of Adam, placed me in the loins of Nuh and then cast me into the loins of Ibrahim. Allah continued to move me from noble loins and pure wombs until He brought me out of my parents. None of them were ever joined together in fornication.'

The famous poem of al-'Abbas in praise of the Prophet, may Allah bless him and grant him peace, testifies to the soundness of this tradition. (*Ash-Shifa'* of *Qadi* 'Iyad: 1.2.6).

And:

Abu Muhammad al-Makki, Abu'l-Layth as-Samaraqandi and others related that when Adam rebelled, he said, 'O Allah, forgive me my error by the right of Muhammad!' Allah said to him, 'How do you know Muhammad?' He said, 'I saw written in every place in the Garden, "There is no god but Allah, Muhammad is the Messenger of Allah," so I knew that he was the most honoured of creation in Your eyes.' So Allah turned to him and forgave him. It is said that this is the interpretation of the words of Allah, **'Adam learned some words from his Lord.'** (2.37).

Another variant has that Adam said, 'When You created me, I lifted my gaze to Your Throne and written on it was: "There is no god but Allah, Muhammad is the Messenger of Allah," so I knew there would be no one held in greater esteem by You than the one whose name You placed alongside Your own Name.' Allah then revealed to him, 'By My might and majesty, he is the last of the Prophets among your descendants. If it had not been for him, I would not have created you.' It is said that Adam was given the *kunya*, Abu Muhammad. Some people say that it was Abu'l-Bashar (father of mankind). (*Ash-Shifa'* of *Qadi* 'Iyad: 1.3.1).

And:

> Abu Salama said that Abu Hurayra said, 'They asked, "Messenger of Allah, when was prophethood decreed for you?" He replied, "When Adam was between the body and the spirit."' (At-Tirmidhi).
>
> Wa'ila ibn al-Asqa' said that the Messenger of Allah said, 'Allah chose Isma'il from the children of Ibrahim. He chose the Banu Kinana from the children of Isma'il. He chose the Quraysh from the Banu Kinana. He chose the Banu Hashim from the Quraysh. He chose me from the Banu Hashim.' (Muslim).
>
> In the *hadith* of Anas, the Prophet said, 'I am the most honoured of the Children of Adam with my Lord and it is no boast.' (At-Tirmidhi).
>
> Then there is the *hadith* of Ibn 'Abbas, 'I am the noblest of the first and the last and it is no boast.' (At-Tirmidhi).
>
> 'A'isha said that the Prophet said, 'Jibril, peace be upon him, came to me and said, "I have searched the East and West of the earth and I saw no man better than Muhammad and I saw no clan better than the Banu Hashim."' (Al-Bayhaqi, Abu Nu'aym and at-Tabarani). (*Ash-Shifa'* of *Qadi* 'Iyad: 1.3.1).

And:

Al-'Irbad ibn Sariyya said that he heard the Messenger of Allah say, 'I am the slave of Allah and the Seal of the Prophets. I was cast into the clay of Adam and was the promise of my father Ibrahim and the good news of 'Isa ibn Maryam.' (Ibn Hanbal, al-Bayhaqi and al-Hakam). (*Ash-Shifa'* of *Qadi* 'Iyad: 1.3.1).

And:

Khalid ibn Ma'dan said that a group of the Companions of the Messenger of Allah said, 'Messenger of Allah, tell us about yourself!' He replied, 'Yes, I will. I am the answer to the supplication of my father, Ibrahim, when He said, **"Our Lord, send among them a Messenger from among them."** (2.129). 'Isa gave good news of me. When my mother was pregnant with me, she dreamt that a light came from her that illuminated the castles of Bosra in Syria. I was suckled among the Banu Sa'd ibn Bakr. While I was out with one of my foster-brothers behind our tents herding some animals of ours, two men wearing white garments came up to me. (One variant has 'three men with a golden basin filled with snow'.). They held me fast and split open my chest from my throat to my lower belly. Then they took out my heart and split it open. Then they extracted a black drop from it and threw it away. Then they washed my heart and chest with that snow until they had cleaned it.' (The same thing is related from Abu Dharr, Shaddad ibn Aws and Anas ibn Malik.).

He said in another *hadith*, 'Then one of them reached for something and there was a ring made of light in his hand which would dazzle anyone who looked at it. He sealed my heart with it and my heart was filled with belief and wisdom. Then he put it back. Then the other one passed his hand over that part of my chest and it was healed. (In one variant, from Ad-Darimi and Abu Nu'aym, Jibril said, 'It is a sturdy heart which has two eyes in it which see and two ears which hear.').

'Then one of them said to his fellow, "Weigh him against ten of his community," so they weighed me against them and I outweighed them. Then he said, "Weigh him against a hundred of his community," so they weighed me against them and I outweighed them. Then he said, "Weigh him against a thousand of his community," so they weighed me against them and I outweighed them. Then he said, "Leave him. If you were to weigh him against all of his community, he would still outweigh them all."

'Then they embraced me and kissed my head and kissed me between my eyes. Then they said, "O beloved, do not fear! If you only knew the blessing that this meant for you, you would be delighted!" Then they said, "How honoured you are with Allah! Allah and His angels are with you."' In Abu Dharr's version of the *hadith*, he said, 'They left me, and I can almost see them still.' (*Ash-Shifa'* of *Qadi* 'Iyad: 1.3.1).

So much is known about the life of *sayyedina* Muhammad and his family and companions, may the blessings and peace of Allah be on him and them, that there is no single book that can contain all that is known about him and them.

The record of *sayyedina* Muhammad's being orphaned at an early age, of his being recognised by Christian monks while still a child, of his becoming noted for his honesty and trustworthiness as a young man, of his marrying his first wife Khadija when he was twenty-five years old, of the children whom she bore for him and what happened to them, of the revelation of the Qur'an beginning when he was forty years old, and of all that subsequently happened during the next twenty-three years – at the end of which the revelation of the Qur'an had been completed, the message delivered, and the *deen* of Islam established in all its simplicity and splendour – the record of all this is well documented and has been meticulously authenticated and need not be repeated here.

It is not possible, within the scope of this book, to do more than make some general observations about the life and qualities of *sayyedina* Muhammad and his family and companions, may the blessings and peace of Allah be on him and them, and to give some indication of his and their high station with Allah: within the context of these pages it is only possible to stand on the shore and describe a little of what can be seen of the ocean – to dive into it is another matter, and up to the reader!

As we have already seen, both *sayyedina* Musa and *sayyedina* 'Isa certainly told their followers about the coming of *sayyedina* Muhammad, and their original revelations, the Taurah and the Ingil, clearly described him. Thus when describing those who believe in the signs of Allah – including the Prophet Muhammad, may Allah bless him and grant him peace – Allah says :

> Those who follow the Messenger, the Prophet who can neither read nor write, whom they will find described in the Taurah and the Ingil which are with them – he will enjoin what is right on them and forbid them what is wrong, and he will make the good things lawful for them and prohibit them the foul things, and he will relieve them of their burden and the chains they used to wear.
>
> So those who believe in him, and honour him, and help him, and follow the light which is sent down with him – they are the successful ones.
>
> Say (O Muhammad): 'O mankind, surely I am the Messenger of Allah – the One to Whom the dominion of the heavens and the earth belongs – to all of you. There is no god except Him – He gives life and He gives death – so believe in Allah and His Messenger, the Prophet who can neither read nor write, who believes in Allah and His words – and follow him so that you may be rightly guided.' (7.157-158).

And, as we have already seen:

> And (remember) when Musa said to his people, 'O my people, why do you persecute me when you well know that I am the Messenger of Allah to you?' So when they went astray Allah sent their hearts astray. And Allah does not guide the people who are evil.
>
> And (remember) when 'Isa son of Maryam said, 'O Tribe of Israel, surely I am the Messenger of Allah to you, confirming what was (revealed) before me in the Torah, and bringing good news of a Messenger who will come after me, whose name is the Praised One (Ahmad).'

('Ahmad' is one of the names of the Prophet Muhammad, may Allah bless him and grant him peace, meaning 'the Most Praiseworthy', 'the One who Distinguishes between Truth and Falsehood', and 'the Comforter'. Its equivalent in Greek is '*Parakletos*' or '*Parakleitos*', meaning 'the Comforter' or 'the Praised One'.)

> Yet when he came to them with clear proofs, they said, 'This is clearly magic.'
>
> And who does greater wrong than the one who makes up a lie against Allah when he is called to Islam? And Allah does not guide people who do wrong.
>
> They desire to put out the Light of Allah with their words, but Allah will perfect His Light however much those who disbelieve detest it.
>
> He it is Who has sent His Messenger with the guidance and the true *deen*, so that He may make it overcome all other religions, however much the idol worshippers detest it.
>
> O you who trust, shall I lead you to a bargain that will save you from a painful punishment? You should believe in Allah and His Messenger, and fight in the way of Allah with your wealth and your selves.
>
> That is better for you, if only you knew.
>
> He will forgive you your wrong actions and bring you into Gardens underneath which rivers flow and pleasant dwellings in Gardens of Eden.
>
> That is the supreme success.
>
> And He will give you something else that you love: Help from Allah and victory that is near – and give good news to the believers!
>
> O you who believe, be Allah's helpers, just as when 'Isa son of Maryam said to the disciples, 'Who will be my helpers for Allah?' and the disciples replied, 'We are Allah's helpers.'
>
> And a party of the Tribe of Israel believed, and a party disbelieved, and We strengthened those who believed against their enemy, and so they became the ones who prevailed. (61.5-14).

As was the case with all of the Messengers before *sayyedina* Muhammad, may the blessings and peace of Allah be on him and them, to begin with only a few believed in him, while many rejected him, as this account which is taken from *The Women of Madina* by Muhammad Ibn Sa'd so clearly demonstrates:

'Afif al-Kindi said, 'During the *Jahiliyya* I came to Makka wishing to purchase clothes and perfume for my family. I stayed with al-'Abbas ibn 'Abdu'l-Muttalib. While I was with him, looking at the Ka'ba when the sun was high, a young man came up to the Ka'ba. He raised his head towards the heaven and concentrated his attention. Then he faced the Ka'ba standing upright. Then a boy came and stood at his right. A woman soon came and stood behind them. Then the young man bowed and the boy and the woman bowed. Then the young man raised his head and the boy and woman raised their heads. Then the young man went into prostration and the boy and woman went into prostration. I said, "'Abbas, I see something immense." Al-'Abbas said, "Something immense. Do you know who this young man is?" I said, "No, I do not know." He said, "This is Muhammad ibn 'Abdullah ibn 'Abdu'l-Muttalib, my nephew. Do you know who this boy is?" I said, "No, I do not know." He said, "'Ali ibn Abi Talib ibn 'Abdu'l-Muttalib, my nephew. Do you know who this woman is?" I said, "No, I do not know." He said, "This is Khadija bint Khuwaylid, the wife of this nephew. This nephew of mine you see tells us that his Lord is the Lord of the heavens and the earth, who enjoined on him this *deen* which he is following. He is following it and, by Allah, I do not know that there is anyone on the face of the earth following this *deen* except these three."'

'Afif said, 'Later I wished I had been their fourth.'

Most of those in Makka who rejected *sayyedina* Muhammad and his first small group of followers were idol worshippers, but there were also communities of both Jews and Christians settled in Arabia who had no desire to have their adopted religions challenged, and who tried to catch the Prophet Muhammad out by asking him questions which they thought he would be unable to answer. Since *sayyedina* Muhammad was illiterate – he could neither read nor write – and since he had never 'studied' any religion or received religious instruction from any Jewish rabbi or Christian priest, he, may Allah bless him and grant him peace, relied entirely on revelation from Allah which took place through the angel Jibril.

On one occasion, when the idol-worshippers of Makka – having sought the advice of the Jews of Khaybar who lived some two hundred miles or so north of Makka – asked him three questions which the Jews said could only be answered by a Prophet, *sayyedina* Muhammad replied that he would give them the answers the next day, but without saying, *'Insh'Allah'* – 'God willing'. As a result, he was not given the answers the next day, and indeed there was a cessation in the revelation of the Qur'an for fifteen days. When the answers were finally revealed – much to the annoyance of those who had suggested the questions as well as of those who had asked them – *sayyedina* Muhammad, may Allah bless him and grant him peace, was gently reprimanded with the following *ayat*:

> **And do not say, 'Surely I will do that tomorrow,' about anything without saying, *'insh'Allah'* – and when you forget, then remember your Lord, and say, 'Perhaps my Lord will guide me nearer to what is right than this.' (18.23-24).**

The three questions which the rabbis had suggested were firstly, to ask *sayyedina* Muhammad about some young men who left their people in the days of old, because they worshipped other than Allah; and secondly, to ask him about a traveller who reached the ends of the earth in the east and in the west; and thirdly, to ask him about the Spirit.

The answer which was revealed concerning the first question – which relates, it has been said, to the story of the seven sleepers of Ephesus who lived, and slept, during the third century CE – and Allah knows best – is to be found in Surat al-Kahf:

> **And do you consider that the people of the cave, and the inscription, were among Our amazing signs? – When the young men sought refuge in the cave and said, 'O our Lord, grant us mercy from Your presence and guide us aright in our affair.'**
>
> **So We sealed up their hearing in the Cave for a number of years, and then We woke them up, so that We might know which of the two parties could best calculate how long they had stayed there.**
>
> **We relate their story to you in truth: surely they were young men who trusted in their Lord, and We increased them in guidance, and We made their hearts firm when they stood up and said, 'Our Lord is the Lord of the heavens and the**

earth – we will never pray to any god instead of Him, for then whatever we said would be a lie!

'These people of ours have chosen other gods instead of Him, even though they have no clear authority – and who is more in the wrong than someone who makes up something about Allah which is a lie?' –

And when you withdraw from them and whatever they worship except Allah, then seek refuge in the cave – your Lord will spread out His mercy for you and deal with you in your affair with ease.

– And you would have seen the sun when it rose moving past their cave on the right, and when it set passing by them on the left, with them in between – that is one of the signs of Allah – whomever Allah guides is rightly guided, and as for whomever He leads astray, you will never find a friend to guide him aright.

And you would have thought that they were awake, even though they were asleep – and We made them turn over, to the right and to the left, with their dog with his forelegs stretched out at the entrance.

And if you had looked at them closely, you would certainly have turned away from them and run, filled with awe of them.

And in the same way We woke them up so that they could question each other. One of them asked, 'How long have you been here?'

(Some of) them replied, 'We have been here for a day, or part of a day.'

(Others) said, 'Your Lord knows best how long you have been here; now let one of you go off to the city with this money of yours, and let him see which food is the purest, and let him bring you a supply of it – and let him be courteous, and let him not tell anyone about you, for if they were to find out about you, they would surely stone you or make you return to their religion – and then you would never be successful.'

And in the same way We revealed who they were (to the people of the city) – when they were arguing amongst themselves about what to do about them – so that they might know that surely the promise of Allah is true, and that surely there is no doubt about the Hour.

And they said, 'Build a dwelling for them – their Lord knows best about them.'

And those who prevailed as to what to do about them said, 'We will certainly build a place of worship for them.'

Some will say there were three of them, with their dog making four, and some will say there were five of them, with their dog making six – guessing at what they do not know – and some will say there were seven of them, with their dog making eight.

Say: 'My Lord knows best how many of them there were, and only a few know a little about them – so do not argue about them except in general discussion, and do not ask any of them to express an opinion about them.'

And do not say, 'Surely I will do that tomorrow,' about anything without saying, *'insh'Allah'* – and when you forget, then remember your Lord, and say, 'Perhaps my Lord will guide me nearer to what is right than this.'

And they were in their cave for three hundred and nine years altogether.

Say: 'Allah knows best how long they were there – the Unseen of the heavens and the earth belongs to Him – how clearly He sees and hears! They did not have any protecting friend other than Him – and He does not have any partner to share in His control.'

So recite what has been inspired in you from the Book of your Lord – there is no one who can change His words, and you will not find any refuge other than Him. (18.9-27).

The answer which was revealed concerning the second question – which relates, it has been said by some, to Alexander the Great – and Allah knows best – is also to be found in Surat al-Kahf:

And they ask you about Dhu'l-Qarnayn.

Say: 'I will tell you what to remember about him.'

Surely We made him powerful in the land, and We gave him the means to (achieve) everything.

And he followed a road until he reached a place in the west where the sun appeared to be setting in a hot spring, and there he found a people.

We said, 'O Dhu'l-Qarnayn, you can either punish them or else treat them kindly.'

He said, 'As for whoever does wrong, we will punish him – and then he will be brought back to his Lord, Who will punish him with a terrible punishment; and as for whoever believes and does good, his reward will be good,' – and We will decree ease for him with Our command.

Then he followed a road until he reached a place in the east, where he found the sun rising on a people for whom We had not provided any shelter from it.

That is how it was – and We certainly encompassed wherever he was in Our knowledge.

Then he followed a road until he reached a pass between two mountains, and on the other side he found a people who could hardly understand a word.

They said, 'O Dhu'l-Qarnayn, surely Yajuj wa Majuj (Gog and Magog) are spreading corruption in the land – so let us pay you tribute on the condition that you set up a barrier between us and them.'

He replied, 'The dominion which my Lord has granted me is better (than any tribute), but if you help me with your strength, I will build a great wall between you and them: Bring me lumps of iron!' – and then, when he had filled in the pass between the sides of the two mountains, he said, 'Blow!' – and then, when he had made it red hot, he said, 'Bring me molten brass to pour over it!'

And they (Yajuj wa Majuj) could not climb over it, and they could not tunnel through it.

> He (Dhu'l-Qarnayn) said, 'This is a mercy from my Lord, but when the promise of my Lord is fulfilled, He will turn it to dust – and the promise of my Lord is always true.'
>
> And on that day, We will leave some of them to surge against others, and then the Trumpet will be blown, and then We shall gather them all together. (18.83-99).

It is interesting to note in passing that some commentators on the Qur'an have pointed out the link between the European Khazar Jews – who as we have already seen in *Volume Two* are not descended from any of the twelve tribes of the Tribe of Israel – and Gog and Magog, the turkic tribe who originally lived in the Caucasus, between the Black sea and the Caspian sea, and from whom King Joseph of the Khazars claimed his ancestry.

It is also interesting to note that the Muslim historian, At-Tabari, relates accounts of at least two expeditions made by the early Muslims to find and examine the wall that was erected by Dhu'l-Qarnayn – who, in the opinion of Ibn Kathir, in his book *Al-Bidayah wa'l-Nihayah – The Beginning and the End*, was a follower of *sayyedina* Ibrahim, peace be on him. D. M. Dunlop refers to these accounts in his book, *The History of the Jewish Khazars*, stating that the wall in question was 'the Caucasus fortification (dating from pre-Islamic times) known as the Wall of Darband', and observing that 'successive courses of bright and dark material (copper and iron) are the most prominent feature of both accounts, which of course may be influenced by the Qur'an passage in which iron and molten brass are mentioned.' Allah knows best.

The answer which was revealed concerning the third question which the idol worshippers of Makka put to *sayyedina* Muhammad, may Allah bless him and grant him peace, is to be found in Surat al-'Isra':

> And they ask you about the *Ruh*.
>
> Say: 'The *Ruh* is by the command of my Lord, and you have only been given a little knowledge about it.'
>
> And if We wanted, We could certainly take away what We have inspired in you – and then you would not find anyone to protect you against us concerning it, unless it was by

the mercy of your Lord – surely His generosity to you has always been tremendous. (17.85-87).

It is interesting to note in passing that *sayyedina* Muhammad, may Allah bless him and grant him peace, could not possibly have known the answers to these three questions until they were revealed to him – and that if he had known them, then he would have given them straight away, instead of enduring the mockery of the idol worshippers for fifteen days.

It is also interesting to note that although the Jews of Khaybar had said that if *sayyedina* Muhammad did answer the questions truthfully then it would mean that he was a Prophet and should be followed, most of them – and most of the idol worshippers who had consulted them – refused to follow him once the answers were forthcoming!

Not long after the episode of the three questions, there followed an event which not only indicated the extent and limits of what little knowledge of the Spirit man is permitted, but which also confirmed the close connection that exists between the Prophet Muhammad and the other Prophets and Messengers, may the blessings and peace of Allah be on him and them: this was the famous – and at times misunderstood – Night Journey of the Prophet Muhammad, may Allah bless him and grant him peace, his *'isra' wa'l-mi'raj*, when he travelled from Makka to Jerusalem on the back of a winged mount called the *Buraq*, did the prayer there with some of the Prophets praying behind him, and then ascended through the seven heavens – meeting some of the earlier Messengers in each of the heavens on the way, and then on – past the limit of forms in the Unseen – to the Presence of Allah.

The following excerpts from the commentary of *Qadi* 'Iyad on the Night Journey are invaluable, since they assist the reader in coming to an understanding of an event which transcends what are commonly accepted as the normal constraints of time and space:

> This concerns his intimate conversation with Allah, his vision, his being *imam* of all the Prophets and his ascent to the Lote-Tree of the Furthest Limit and what he saw of the greatest signs of his Lord during his Night Journey.

One of his special qualities is revealed by the story of the Night Journey and the exalted degrees that were conferred on him by it. It is mentioned in the Mighty Book and there are commentaries on it in sound *hadith*.

Allah says, **'Glory be to the One who travelled at night with His slave from the Masjid al-Haram to the Further Mosque whose precincts We have blessed that We might show him some of Our signs. He is the Hearing, the Seeing.'** (17.1).

And, **'By the Star when it falls, your comrade is not astray nor does he err. This is only a revelation revealed, taught him by one terrible in power, strong (Jibril). He stood poised on the higher horizon, then drew near and hung suspended, two bows' lengths away or nearer, then He revealed to his servant what He revealed. His heart does not lie about what it saw. What, will you dispute with him about what he sees? He saw him another time by the Lote-Tree of the Furthest Limit near which is the garden of the Refuge when there covered the Lote-Tree that which covered it. His eye did not swerve nor sweep aside. Indeed, he saw one of the greatest signs of his Lord.'** (53.1-18).

The Muslims do not doubt that his Night Journey is true since it is written in the Qur'an and many and widespread *hadiths* have reported its details and commented on its marvels and the special qualities of our Prophet, Muhammad, it demonstrates. We think that the most complete version of it has already been given but we will indicate a little more about it.

Anas ibn Malik said that the Messenger of Allah said, 'The *Buraq* was brought to me. It was a white animal somewhat taller than a donkey, but smaller than a mule. Its step covered a distance equal to the range of its vision. I mounted it and rode until I was brought to Jerusalem. Then I tied it to the ring which the Prophets use. Then I entered the mosque and prayed two *rak'ats* there. I came out and Jibril brought me a vessel of milk and a vessel of wine. I chose the milk and Jibril said, "You have chosen the *fitra*."

'Then he went up with me to the first heaven. Jibril asked for it to be opened and a voice said, "Who is it?" He replied, "Jibril." The voice said, "Who is with you?" He replied, "Muhammad." It said, "Was he sent for?" He replied, "He was sent for," and the door opened for us. I found Adam who welcomed me and prayed for me.

'Then we went up to the second heaven and Jibril asked for it to be opened. A voice said, "Who is it?" He replied, "Jibril." It said, "Who is with you?" He replied, "Muhammad." It said, "Was he sent for?" He replied, "He was," and the door was opened for us. There I found my cousins, 'Isa ibn Maryam and Yahya ibn Zakariyya. They welcomed me and prayed for me.

'Then we went up to the third heaven and the same thing happened. It was opened for me and there was Yusuf. He had been given half of all beauty. He welcomed me and prayed for me.

'Then we went up to the fourth heaven and the same thing happened. I found Idris, and he welcomed me and prayed for me. Allah has said, **"We raised him up to a high place."** (19.57).

'Then we went up to the fifth heaven and the same thing happened. There was Harun, who welcomed me and prayed for me.

'Then we went up to the sixth heaven and the same thing happened. There I found Musa, who welcomed me and prayed for me.

'Then we went up to the seventh heaven and the same thing happened. There I found Ibrahim leaning against the Frequented House (*Al-Bayt al-Ma'mur*). Every day, seventy thousand angels enter into it and do not emerge.

'Then he took me to the Lote-Tree of the Furthest Limit whose leaves are like the ears of elephants and whose fruits are like earthenware vessels. When a command from Allah covers it, what is covered undergoes a change which no creature is capable of describing due to its sublime beauty.

'Then Allah revealed to me what He revealed and He made fifty prayers every day and night obligatory for me. I came down to Musa and he asked, "What did your Lord make obligatory for your people?" I replied, "Fifty prayers." He said, "Go back to your Lord and ask Him to lighten it. Your community will never be able to do that. I have tested the Banu Isra'il and know by experience."

'So I went back to my Lord and said, "My Lord, lighten it for my community!" so He deducted five prayers. I went back to Musa and said, "He deducted five for me." He said, "Your community will not be able to do that, so go back and ask Him to lighten it."

'I kept going back and forth between my Lord and Musa until Allah said, "Muhammad, they are five prayers every day and night. Each prayer counts as ten, so that makes fifty prayers. Whoever intends to do something good, and then does not do it, a good action will be written for him. If he does it, then ten will be written for him. Whoever intends to do something bad and does not do it, nothing will be written against him. If he does it, then one bad action will be recorded."

'Then I went down to Musa and told him about that. He said, "Go back to your Lord and ask Him to lighten it."' The Messenger of Allah said, 'I have gone back to my Lord so often that I am ashamed before Him.' (Muslim).

Yunus related from Ibn Shihab from Anas that Abu Dharr said that the Messenger of Allah said, 'The roof of my house was split open and Jibril descended and opened my breast. Then he washed it with water from Zamzam. Then he brought a gold dish filled with wisdom and belief and he poured it into my breast and then closed it up. He took me by the hand and ascended with me to heaven.' (Al-Bukhari and Muslim).

Qatada related a similar *hadith* from Anas from Malik ibn Sa'sa'a which puts things in a different order and has different details and a different order of the Prophets in the heavens. Thabit's *hadith* is better and more precise. There are some additions to the Night Journey and I will mention some of the useful points in them.

In the hadith of Ibn Shihab we find, 'Every Prophet said to me, "Welcome to the right-acting Prophet and right-acting brother," except for Adam and Ibrahim who said "a right-acting son".'

Ibn 'Abbas has, 'Then he went up with me until I came to a level plain where I heard the squeaking of pens.' Anas has, 'Then he went up with me until I came to the Lote-Tree of the Furthest Limit. It was covered in colours that I did not recognise. Then I was brought into the Garden.'

In the *hadith* of Malik ibn Sa'sa'a we find, 'When I passed Musa, he wept. He was asked, "Why are you weeping?" He replied, "Lord, this is a young man who was sent after me and more of his community will enter the Garden than those of my community."' (Al-Bukhari and Muslim).

In the *hadith* of Abu Hurayra we find, 'I saw myself in a group of the Prophets. When the time for the prayer came, I was their *imam.* Someone said, "Muhammad! This is Malik, the guardian of the Fire, so greet him." I turned around and he greeted me first.' (Al-Bayhaqi).

In the *hadith* of Abu Hurayra we find, 'Then he travelled until he came to Jerusalem and dismounted. He tied his mount to the Rock and prayed with the angels. When the prayer was over, they asked, "Jibril, who is this with you?" He said, "This is Muhammad, the Messenger of Allah and the Seal of the Prophets." They asked, "Has he been sent already?" He said, "Yes." They said, "May Allah give him long life as a brother and a *khalif*! An excellent brother! An excellent *khalif*!" Then he met the spirits of the Prophets who praised their Lord and he mentioned what each of them said. They were: Ibrahim, Musa, 'Isa, Da'ud, and Sulayman.'

He continued, 'Muhammad praised his Lord, the Mighty and Majestic, saying, "All of you have praised your Lord, so I will praise Him. Praise be to Allah Who has sent me as a mercy to the worlds and as a bringer of good news and a warner for all people. He has sent down the *Furqan* ('the Discrimination', one of the names of the Qur'an) on me which makes all things clear. He has made my community the best community and He has made my community a middle community. They are the first and they are the last. He opened my breast for me and removed my burden from me and elevated my renown and made me an opener and a seal." Ibrahim said, "This is why Muhammad is better than you."'

In the *hadith* of Ibn Mas'ud we find, 'He brought me to the Lote-Tree of the Furthest Limit which is in the sixth heaven. What rises from the earth to it reaches and touches part of it. What falls from above it reaches it and touches part of it. Allah says, **"What covers the Lote-Tree covers it."'** (53.16).

In the version of Abu Hurayra through ar-Rabi' ibn Anas we find, 'I was told, "This is the Lote-Tree of the Furthest Limit. Each member of your community who travels your path will reach it. It is the Furthest Lote-Tree. From its roots issue rivers of sweet water, rivers of unaltered milk, rivers of wine to delight the drinkers, and rivers of pure honey. This tree is so immense that it would take a rider seventy years to ride across its shadow. A single leaf from it would shade creation. Light covers it and angels cover it."' Abu Hurayra said that this refers to His words, **'What covers the Lote-Tree covers it.'** (53.16).

Allah said to him, 'Ask!'

Muhammad said, 'You took Ibrahim for a close friend and You gave him an immense kingdom. You spoke directly to Musa. You gave Da'ud an immense kingdom and made iron malleable for him and subjected the mountains to him. You gave Sulayman an immense kingdom and You subjugated to him men, *jinn*, *shaytans*, and the winds and gave him a kingdom that no one after him would have. You taught 'Isa the Taurah and the Ingil, and You let him heal the blind and the leper, and You protected him and his mother from the accursed *shaytan* so that he would find no way against them.'

Allah said to him, 'I have taken you as a close friend and a beloved. Written in the Torah is: "Muhammad is the Beloved of the Merciful." I have sent you to all people and I have made your community such that none will be permitted to speak until they have testified that you are My slave and My Messenger. I made you the first of the Prophets to be created and the last of them to be sent. I gave you the seven *Mathani* and I did not give them to any Prophet before you. I gave you the seals of the Surat al-Baqara from a treasure under My Throne, and I did not give them to any Prophet before you. I have made you an opener and a seal.'

Another version has: 'The Messenger of Allah was given three things: he was given the five prayers; he was given the seals of Surat al-Baqara; and he was given pardon for the major wrong actions of everyone of his community who did not associate anything with Allah.' (Muslim). Allah says, **'The heart did not lie about what it saw.' (53.11)**. Ibn Mas'ud says that he saw Jibril in his true form which had six hundred wings.

The *hadith* of Sharik ibn Abi Namr says that he saw Musa in the seventh heaven. He was taken higher than that to what only Allah knows. Musa said, 'I did not think that anyone would ever be raised above me.'

Anas said that the Prophet prayed with the Prophets in Jerusalem.

Anas said that the Messenger of Allah said, "One day while I was sitting, Jibril came and struck me between my shoulders. I got up and went up to a tree in which there was something which resembled two birds' nests. He sat in one and I sat in the other. It grew until it filled the east and west. Had I so wished, I could have touched the sky. Looking around, I glanced at Jibril and it seemed as if he was a piece of transparent cloth. I recognised the superiority of his knowledge of Allah over mine. The gate of heaven was opened and I saw a blinding light and the veil dropped below me. The pearl and the ruby split open, and then Allah revealed to me what He wished to reveal.' (Al-Bazzar and al-Bayhaqi).

Al-Bazzar mentioned that 'Ali ibn Abi Talib said, 'When Allah wanted to teach His Messenger the *adhan*, Jibril came to him with a riding beast called the *Buraq*. He went to mount it and it shied away from him. Jibril said, "Be still. By Allah, no slave more honoured with Allah than Muhammad has ever ridden you." So he mounted it and rode until it brought him to the veil just below the Merciful. Then an angel came out of the veil and the Messenger of Allah asked, "Jibril! Who is this?" He said, "By the One Who sent you with the truth, I have the closest station of all creatures to Allah, but I have not seen this angel from the time I was created until this very minute." The angel said, "Allah is greater! Allah is greater!" A voice came from behind the veil, "My slave has spoken the truth. I am greater! I am greater!" The angel said, "I testify that there is no god but Allah." A voice from behind the veil said, "My slave has spoken the truth. There is no god but Me,"' and the rest of the *adhan* is mentioned, although he did not mention the response to the words, 'Come to the prayer, come to success.'

He said, 'Then the angel took Muhammad by the hand and advanced him so that he was the *Imam* of the inhabitants of the heavens, including Adam and Nuh.'

Abu Ja'far Muhammad ibn 'Ali ibn al-Husayn said, 'Allah honoured Muhammad above the inhabitants of the heavens and the earth. (Al-Bazzar).

The veil is for creatures, not for the Creator. They are veiled. The Creator – may He be magnified – is disconnected from anything that could veil Him since veils are defined by the senses. He veils the eyes, the inner eyes, and the perception of His creatures how and when He wills as He has said, **'No, on the day they are veiled from their Lord.' (83.15).**

In this *hadith*, it says, 'Then an angel came out of the veil,' so it must be that it is a veil which veils what is beyond it so that the angels cannot perceive His power, immensity, and the marvels of His *Malakut* and *Jabarut* beyond that point. This indicates that this veil is not particular to the Essence. What Ka'b said in his commentary on the Lote-Tree of the Furthest Limit indicates this: 'The knowledge of the angels ends there. There they find the command of Allah and their knowledge does not pass beyond that point.'

As for 'below the Merciful', it can be considered that what is connected to it has been omitted, i.e. below the Throne of the Merciful, or one of His immense signs or the bases of the realities of His gnoses, as He knows best. It is similar to the words of Allah, **'Ask the village,'** (12.82), meaning its people.

It says, 'A voice came from behind the veil, "My slave has spoken the truth. I am greater! I am greater!"' The literal meaning of this is that he does not hear Allah's words here, but from behind a veil as Allah says, **'It is not for any mortal that Allah should speak to him except by revelation or from behind a veil, or that He should send a Messenger to reveal whatever He will, by His leave. He is High, Wise.'** (42.51). This means he does not see Him. His eye is veiled from seeing Him.

If the statement, 'Muhammad, may Allah bless him and grant him peace, saw his Lord, the Mighty and Majestic,' is true, it is possible that that occurred in another place before or after this and at that time the veil was lifted from his eye so that he saw Him. Allah knows best. (*Ash-Shifa'* of *Qadi* 'Iyad: 1.3.2).

Having summarised the three positions that have been taken by the commentators – as to whether the Prophet Muhammad, may Allah bless him and grant him peace, went on His Night Journey in spirit in a true dream, or in his physical body while he was awake, or in his body while awake from Makka to Jerusalem and then in spirit through the seven heavens – Qadi 'Iyad concludes:

> The true, sound position in this, Allah willing, is that the Night Journey was both in spirit and in body throughout the entire event. The Qur'anic verses, sound traditions and considered opinion all indicate this. One does not abandon the truth of the literal meaning for interpretation except when nothing else is possible. That he went on the Night Journey in body while awake is not impossible. If it had been a dream, Allah would have said, 'with the *spirit* of His slave'. Allah also says, **'The eye did not swerve nor did it sweep away.'** (53.17).

If it had only been a dream, then it would not have involved either a sign or a miracle. The unbelievers would not have thought it impossible and rejected it and the weak Muslims would not have been doubtful about it and found it a test since things like this are not unknown in dreams. This doubt only arose because they knew that his report indicated it being in his physical body while awake, including what he mentioned about praying with the Prophets in Jerusalem or in the heavens, Jibril bringing him the *Buraq*, the ascension, asking for the heavens to open and it being said, 'Who is it?' and the answer 'Muhammad' being given, his meeting the Prophets there and what happened with them and their welcome to him, the obligation of the prayer being confirmed and his going back and forth to Musa. Ibn 'Abbas said, 'It was direct vision which he saw with his own eyes. It was not a dream.'

Al-Hasan al-Basri said that the Prophet said, 'While I was sleeping in the *Hijr*, Jibril came to me and prodded me with his foot. I sat up but I did not see anything so I lay back down again.' That happened three times. He said, 'The third time, he grabbed me by the arm and pulled me to the door of the mosque. There was the riding animal, the *Buraq*.'

Umm Hani' said, 'The Messenger of Allah was taken on the Night Journey the night he was in my house. He had prayed the final night prayer and slept with us. At the time of *fajr*, the Messenger of Allah woke us up. Then he prayed *subh* with us. He said, "Umm Hani'! I prayed the final night prayer with you, as you saw, in this valley, then I went to Jerusalem and prayed there. Then I prayed the morning prayer with you as you see."' (Ibn Ishaq, at-Tabarani and Ibn Jarir). This makes it clear that he went in his physical body.

Abu Bakr said that he said to the Prophet about the night of the Night Journey, 'Messenger of Allah, I looked for you in your place but I did not find you.' The Prophet replied, 'Jibril carried me to the Furthest Mosque.' (Al-Bayhaqi and Ibn Mardawayh).

'Umar said that the Messenger of Allah said, 'I prayed in the front of the mosque on the evening of the Night Journey and then came to the Rock in Jerusalem. An angel was standing there with three vessels.' (Ibn Mardawayh).

These are explicit statements which are clear and not impossible, so the literal meaning is taken.

Abu Dharr said that the Prophet said, 'The roof of my house was split open while I was in Makka. Jibril came down and opened my breast and washed it with Zamzam water ... Then he took me by the hand and ascended with me.' (Al-Bukhari and Muslim).

Anas said that the Prophet said, 'I was fetched and they took me to Zamzam and opened my breast.'

Abu Hurayra said that the Prophet said, 'I saw myself in the *Hijr* when Quraysh were asking me about my Night Journey. They asked me about things about which I was not sure, so I was more distressed than I have ever been. Then Allah made it appear before me so that I could look at it.' (Muslim).

The same is related from Jabir. (Al-Bukhari and Muslim).

'Umar ibn al-Khattab related in the *hadith* of the Night Journey that the Prophet said, 'I returned to Khadija and she had not yet turned over.' (*Ash-Shifa'* of *Qadi* 'Iyad: 1.3.3).

Having refuted any possible further arguments that the Night Journey might have been a dream, *Qadi* 'Iyad then considers the vision of his Lord which *sayyedina* Muhammad, may Allah bless him and grant him peace, was granted:

The Early Community disagreed about this. 'A'isha rejected it out of hand, and when Masruq asked her, 'Umm al-Mu'minin! Did Muhammad see his Lord?' she replied, 'My hair is standing on end at what you have said,' and she repeated it three times. 'Whoever told you that has lied. Whoever told you that Muhammad saw his Lord has lied.' Then she recited, **'The eyes do not perceive Him but He perceives the eyes. He is the Subtle, the Aware.'** (6.103). (Al-Bukhari, Muslim, at-Tirmidhi and an-Nasa'i). Some people agree with what A'i'sha said, and it is well-known that Ibn Mas'ud and Abu Hurayra said similar things, stating that it was Jibril he saw. However, this is disputed.

Certain of the *hadith* scholars, theologians and the *fuqaha* reject this statement and the prohibition on the Prophet seeing Allah in this world. Ibn 'Abbas said, 'He saw Him with his eyes,' while 'Ata' related from him that he saw Him with his heart. Abu'l-'Aliyya said that he saw Him with his heart twice. Ibn Ishaq mentioned that Ibn 'Umar sent to Ibn 'Abbas to ask him whether Muhammad had seen his Lord. He replied, 'Yes.' The best known opinion is that he saw his Lord with his eye. This is related from him by various paths of transmission. He said that Allah singled out Musa for direct speech, Ibrahim for close friendship and Muhammad for the vision. The proof of it lies in the words of Allah, **'The heart did not lie about what it saw. What, will you dispute with him about what he sees? He saw Him another time.'** (53.11-13).

Al-Mawardi said, 'It is said that Allah divided His vision and His speech between Musa and Muhammad. Muhammad saw Him twice and He spoke directly to Musa twice.'

Abu'l-Fath ar-Razi and Abu'l-Layth as-Samarqandi relate this from Ka'b al-Ahbar, and 'Abdullah ibn al-Harith said that Ibn 'Abbas and Ka'b agreed on this point. Ibn 'Abbas said, 'As for us, the Banu Hashim, we say that Muhammad saw his Lord twice.' Ka'b said, 'Allah is greater!' until the mountains echoed him. He further said, 'Allah divided His vision and His speech between Muhammad and Musa. He spoke directly to Musa twice and Muhammad saw Him with his heart.'

Sharik relates that when Abu Dharr commented on this *ayah*, he said, 'The Prophet, may Allah bless him and grant him peace, saw his Lord.' As-Samarqandi relates from Muhammad ibn Ka'b al-Qurdhi and Rabi' ibn Anas that the Prophet was asked, 'Have you seen your Lord?' He said, 'I saw Him with my heart, but I did not see Him with my eye.' Malik ibn Yukhamir related from Mu'adh ibn Jabal that the Prophet said, 'I saw my Lord and He asked me, "Muhammad, about what did the Higher Assembly (the angels) disagree?"' (Ibn Hanbal and at-Tirmidhi).

'Abdu'r-Razzaq ibn Hammam related that Hasan al-Basri used to swear by Allah that Muhammad saw his Lord. Abu 'Umar at-Talamanki related this from 'Ikrima. One of the theologians related this position from Ibn Mas'ud. Ibn Ishaq related that Marwan ibn al-Hakam asked Abu Hurayra, 'Did Muhammad see his Lord?' and he replied, 'Yes.'

An-Naqqash related that Ahmad ibn Hanbal said, 'I say that the *hadith* of Ibn 'Abbas means that he saw Him with his eye. He saw Him. He saw Him.' He kept repeating that until he ran out of breath.

Abu 'Umar at-Talamanki said that Ahmad ibn Hanbal said that he saw Him with his heart. He shrank from saying that he saw Him with his eyes in this world.

Sa'id ibn Jubayr said, 'I do not say that he saw Him nor that he did not see Him.'

There is some disagreement between Ibn 'Abbas, 'Ikrima, al-Hasan al-Basri and Ibn Mas'ud in their interpretations of the *ayah*. It is related from Ibn 'Abbas and 'Ikrima, 'He saw Him with his heart.' Al-Hasan al-Basri and Ibn Mas'ud said, 'He saw Jibril.' 'Abdullah ibn Ahmad ibn Hanbal related that his father said, 'He saw Him.'

Ibn 'Ata' relates that Allah's words, **'Did We not expand your breast for you?'** (94.1) mean that He expanded his breast for the vision while He expanded Musa's breast for direct speech.

Abu'l-Hasan 'Ali ibn Isma'il al-Ash'ari and a group of his companions said that he saw Allah with his physical eyes. They said, 'Every Prophet is given a sign. Our Prophet was also given one. He was singled out among them by being given the vision.' One of the *shaykhs* hesitated about this and said, 'There is no clear proof for it, although it is permitted for it to be so.'

The undoubted truth is that it is conceivable for him to have seen Him in this world. There is nothing which makes it logically impossible. The proof that it is permitted in this world lies in the fact that Musa asked for it. It is impossible for a Prophet not to know what is permitted for Allah and what is permitted for himself. He would only ask for something permitted not something impossible. However, the actual event and his witnessing is from the realm of the Unseen about which none has any knowledge except someone who is taught it by Allah.

Allah says, **'You will not see Me, but look at the mountain. If it stays firm in its place, then you will see Me,'** (7.143) meaning you will not be able to bear My vision. Then He made an example for Musa of something stronger and even firmer than his own physical form – the mountain. This does not mean that it is impossible to see Him in this world. In principle, it is feasible. There is no decisive proof in the *Shari'a* that it is impossible or forbidden since it is feasible to see any existent thing, not impossible. There is no proof for the one who says that it is forbidden by the words of Allah, **'The eyes do not perceive Him,'** (6.103) since there are different interpretations of this *ayah* and since, as has already been said, the qualification of the one who says 'in this world' does not necessitate the vision of Allah being impossible.

Certain people have used this *ayah* itself as a proof that it is permitted to see Him, and that, in principle, it is not impossible. Some say that it is the eyes of the unbelievers which do not perceive Him. Some say that, **'The eyes do not perceive Him,'** (6.103) means they do not encompass Him, as Ibn 'Abbas has said. Others say that the eyes do not perceive Him, but those with inner sight do perceive him. None of these interpretations mean that vision is forbidden or impossible.

Equally, there is no real proof in the words of Allah, **'You will not see Me,'** and, **'I have turned to You, and I am the first of the believers,' (7.143)** – (Musa turned to Allah in repentance because of his request to see Allah) – because, as we have already stated, such statements as these do not constitute a general prohibition. The first of the statements is further said to mean, 'You will not see Me *in this world.*' This is an interpretation. Furthermore, there is no text forbidding the vision and the *ayah* refers specifically to Musa. Since there are various interpretations and mere probabilities dominate the case, no definitive statement can be reached. His words, 'I have turned to You in repentance,' mean from asking for what I cannot have.

Abu Bakr al-Hudhali said that, **'You will not see Me,' (7.143)** means it is not for a mortal to be able to look at Me in this world. Whoever looks at Me dies.

I have seen that some of the Early Community and later people thought that it meant that seeing Him in this world is forbidden due to the weakness of people's bodily structure and faculties in this world. These faculties are liable to mishap and destruction. Therefore, they do not have the capacity for the vision of Allah. However, in the Next World, people will have a different structure and will be given more durable faculties and the lights of their inner eyes and hearts will be illuminated. They will then have the strength to bear the vision. Malik ibn Anas said something similar to this: 'He is not seen in this world because He is Enduring. The Enduring cannot be seen by the passing. In the Next World they will be provided with enduring eyes, so the Enduring will be seen by the enduring.'

These are excellent words, but they do not contain any proof that vision is impossible except in respect of the weakness of the faculties. If Allah strengthens whomever He wills among His slaves and gives him the power to bear the vision, then it is not forbidden for him. The power of the sight of Musa and Muhammad has already been mentioned and their perception was accomplished by a divine power which they had been given so that they could perceive what they perceived and see what they saw. Allah knows best.

Qadi Abu Bakr al-Baqillani mentions in the course of his answers about this *ayah* that it means that Musa saw Allah and that is why he fell down in a swoon. The mountain saw its Lord and became dust as the result of a special perception Allah created for it.

He derives that – and Allah knows best – from His words, **'But look at the mountain. If it remains, then you will see Me.'** (7.143). Then He says, **'When his Lord manifested Himself to the mountain, He made it dust and Musa fell down in a swoon.'** (7.143). His manifestation to the mountain was His appearance to Musa so that, according to this statement, he actually saw Him.

Ja'far ibn Muhammad said that He distracted him with the mountain so that He could manifest Himself. If it had not been for that, he would have died in his swoon without recovering. He says that this indicates that Musa saw Him. One of the commentators said he saw the mountain. Seeing the mountain is used as a proof by those who say that Muhammad, our Prophet, saw Allah since it is a proof that it is permissible. It is undoubtedly permissible since there is nothing in the *ayah* to forbid it.

As for the vision being necessary for our Prophet and the statement that he saw Him with his eyes, there is nothing to forbid this. One must rely on these two *ayat* of the Surah of the Star: **'His heart did not lie about what he saw. What, will you dispute with him about what he sees?'** (53.11-12) along with the discussion about them which has already been mentioned earlier. It is possible to say what they probably mean, but there is no definitive tradition transmitted from the Prophet regarding this matter.

The report of Ibn 'Abbas concerns his own belief and does not have an *isnad* going back to the Prophet so it is not necessary to act on what he believes the *ayat* contain. It is the same with the *hadith* of Abu Dharr giving his commentary on the *ayat*. The *hadith* of Mu'adh is open to interpretation and both its *isnad* and text are inadequate.

The other *hadith* of Abu Dharr has various versions and is obscure. One rescension has, 'A light which I saw.' One of our *shaykhs* related that he said, 'I saw Him luminous.' Another version has, 'I asked him and he said, "I saw a light."' It is not possible to use any of these versions as a proof for the validity of the vision. If the sound version is, 'I saw a light,' then he is reporting that he did *not* see Allah. He saw a light and was therefore prevented from seeing Allah. This is what his words, 'A light which I saw,' refer to – how he saw Him with the veil of light which obscures the sight. This is similar to another *hadith*, 'His veil of light.' Another *hadith* has, 'I did not see Him with my eye, I saw Him with my heart.' Then he recited, **'Then he drew near and hung suspended.' (53.8)**.

Allah is able to create in the heart the perception which normally belongs to the eye or however else He wishes. There is no god but Him. If a *hadith* with a clear text had been related about the subject, it would be believed and relied on since there is no absolute impossibility that it could occur. Allah gives success to what is correct. (*Ash-Shifa'* of *Qadi* 'Iyad: 1.3.5).

Elsewhere in his *Ash-Shifa'*, Qadi 'Iyad emphasises the point that this is a zone of knowledge which is beyond words and accordingly it is incapable of verbal description and explanation:

What Allah disclosed to him of His unseen dominion (*jabarut*) and what he saw of the wonders of the angelic worlds (*malakut*) cannot be expressed in words, and the human intellect would not be able to withstand hearing even the least part of it. Allah indicates it by indirect allusion and reference, which shows the esteem in which the Prophet is held. Allah says, **'He revealed to His slave what He revealed.' (53.10)**. This sort of address is called insinuation and subtle indication by the scholars of criticism and rhetoric. According to them it is the most eloquent form of expression.

Allah says, **'He saw one of the greatest signs of his Lord.' (53.18)**. Ordinary understanding is not able to grasp the details of what was revealed and becomes lost in the attempt to define what that great sign really was. (*Ash-Shifa'* of *Qadi* 'Iyad: 1.1.5).

Qadi 'Iyad then goes on to consider the Prophet Muhammad's conversing intimately with Allah, may Allah bless him and grant him peace, indicating what it is possible to indicate:

As regards his conversing intimately with Allah during the Night Journey as is indicated by His words, **'He revealed to His slave what He revealed,'** (53.10) and the contents of various *hadiths*, most of the commentators say that the One Who revealed was Allah to Jibril, and then Jibril revealed it to Muhammad.

There are some who differ from this opinion. Ja'far ibn Muhammad as-Sadiq said, 'He revealed to him without any intermediary.' Something similar is stated by al-Wasiti. Some of the *mutakallimun*, including al-Ash'ari, believe that Muhammad spoke to His Lord during the Night Journey. They relate this from Ibn Mas'ud and Ibn 'Abbas. Others reject this. An-Naqqash mentioned a narration from Ibn 'Abbas that the Prophet said about the words of Allah, **'He drew near and hung suspended,'** (53.8) 'Jibril raised me up and sounds were cut off from me so that I could not hear them. Then I heard my Lord say, "Calm your terror, Muhammad. Draw near, draw near."'

The discussion centres on the words of Allah, **'It is not for any mortal that Allah should speak to him except by revelation or from behind a veil or He sends a Messenger and he reveals what He wills with His permission.' (42.51).**

They say that this consists of three categories:

(1) From behind a veil, as when He spoke to Musa.

(2) By sending angels, as is the case with all the Prophets, and most of the time with our Prophet.

(3) The third category lies in His words, **'revealed to His slave what He revealed,'** (53.10). The only form of speech which remains is direct speech with witnessing. It is said that this 'revelation' is what He cast into the heart of the Prophet without any intermediary.

And:

It is permissible for Allah to speak to Muhammad, may Allah bless him and grant him peace, and whichever of His Prophets He singles out, and it is not beyond the bounds of reason. There is nothing in the *Shari'a* which definitively forbids that. If there was a sound tradition about this, it would be relied on.

That Allah spoke to Musa is true. There is a definitive text concerning it in the Qur'an and it is grammatically emphasised. According to what has been related in *hadith*, Allah elevated

Musa's position to the seventh heaven because He spoke to him. He raised Muhammad up above this until he reached a level plain where he heard the scratching of pens. How then can it be said to be impossible or unlikely for him to have heard speech in this way? Glory be to the One Who singles out whomever He chooses for what He wills and raises some above others in degree. (*Ash-Shifa'* of Qadi 'Iyad: 1.3.6).

Qadi 'Iyad then goes on to consider the Prophet Muhammad's 'drawing near' to Allah, may Allah bless him and grant him peace, making it clear that this is not a question of physical proximity and distance – since, **'The East and the West belong to Allah and wherever you look – there is the face of Allah – surely Allah is All-Present, All-Knowing,'** (2.115) and, **'We are closer to him than his jugular vein'** (50.16) – but rather of spiritual nearness and intimacy:

> As for what is related in the *hadith* of the Night Journey and the literal statement of the *ayat* about drawing near and proximity, **'He drew near and hung suspended and was two bows' lengths away or nearer,** (53.8-9) most commentators say that the 'drawing near' and 'hanging suspended' either refer to Muhammad and Jibril, or are particular to one of them rather than the other, or refer to the Lote-Tree of the Furthest Limit. Ar-Razi and Ibn 'Abbas say that it is Muhammad who drew near and hung suspended near his Lord. Makki and al-Mawardi relate from Ibn 'Abbas that it is the Lord who drew near to Muhammad and lowered Himself to him, i.e. His command and judgement did.
>
> An-Naqqash relates that al-Hasan said, 'He drew near to His slave, Muhammad, and hung there and came close to him. Then He showed him what He wished to show him of His power and immensity.'
>
> Ibn 'Abbas said, 'It is both forward and back. The Carpet drew near to Muhammad on the evening of the Night Journey and he sat on it. Then it went up and he drew near to his Lord. He said, "Jibril raised me up and sounds were cut off from me and I heard the words of my Lord, the Mighty and Majestic."'
>
> We find from Anas in the *Sahih*, 'Jibril ascended with him to the Lote-Tree of the Furthest Limit and the Majestic Lord of Might drew near and hung suspended until He was the distance of two bows' lengths from him or nearer.' Then He re-

vealed to him what He wished and He revealed the fifty prayers to him.

Muhammad ibn Ka'b said, 'Muhammad drew near his Lord, and the distance was two bows' lengths.' Ja'far ibn Muhammad as-Sadiq said, 'His Lord brought him near Him something like two bows' lengths.'

Ja'far ibn Muhammad said, 'Allah's 'drawing near' has no definition or limit. The slave's 'drawing near' is limited.'

He also said, "Howness' cannot be applied to 'drawing near'.' Don't you see how Jibril was veiled from His 'drawing near'? Muhammad drew near to the gnosis and belief in his own heart. He was suspended near by his heart's tranquillity with what drew him near. Doubt and hesitation were removed from his heart.'

Know that what is said about drawing near and nearness to or from Allah has nothing to do with nearness of place or proximity in space. As we mentioned from Ja'far as-Sadiq, "Howness' cannot be applied to 'drawing near'.' The Prophet's drawing near to his Lord and his nearness to Him is made clear by his position, the honour of his rank, the splendour of the lights of his gnosis, and his witnessing the secrets of Allah's unseen world and His power. From Allah to him came kindness, intimacy, expansion and generosity.

Interpretation has to be employed here as with his words, 'Our Lord descends to the nearest heaven', since one of the aspects of descent (*nuzul*) is the granting of favours, kind behaviour, acceptance and kindliness. Al-Wasiti said, 'Whoever speculates that the Prophet himself drew near sees this in terms of distance. All that draws near to the Real hangs in the distance, i.e. far from the perception of its reality since the Real has neither nearness nor distance.'

He said, **'two bows' lengths away or nearer,'** (53.9). Whoever makes the pronoun refer to Allah and not to Jibril in this *ayah*, makes it a statement about the limit of nearness, the subtleness of the place, clarification of gnosis, and honour for Muhammad. It refers to the fulfilling of his desire, the granting of his request, and the extending to him of a warm welcome and the increase of his position and rank from Allah.

It can be interpreted in the same way as His words, 'When he draws near Me by a handspan, I draw near him an arm-span.

Whoever comes to Me walking, I come to him running.' (*Hadith qudsi* in Al-Bukhari). (*Ash-Shifa'* of Qadi 'Iyad: 1.3.7).

When the Prophet Muhammad, may Allah bless him and grant him peace, described his Night Journey to the people of Makka, it strengthened the belief of those who trusted him, and increased the disbelief of those who rejected him, even though he accurately described Jerusalem – which he had never visited before – and even though he described the place between Jerusalem and Makka where he had stopped to have a drink, and even though he described the approaching caravans which he had flown over on his way back from Jerusalem, saying where they were and when they should be arriving in Makka – which they did.

Although the Prophet Muhammad, may Allah bless him and grant him peace, was given many miracles by Allah – particularly regarding the manifesting of food and water out of the Unseen when they were in short supply – there can be no doubt that the greatest miracle which was given to him was the Qur'an, since as we have already seen, he was illiterate and could neither read nor write. *Qadi 'Iyad* writes:

> Abu Hurayra said that the Prophet said, 'Every Prophet has been given signs by which people will believe in him, and what I have been given is the revelation which Allah has revealed to me, and I hope that I will have the greatest number of followers on the Day of Rising.' (Al-Bukhari and Muslim).
>
> According to scholars, this means that his miracle will continue as long as this world remains. All the miracles of the Prophets vanished after a time and were only seen by those who were present during their time. The Qur'an will remain generation after generation as something that can be seen by the eye, not just as information, and it will remain until the Day of Rising. This is a simplified discussion of a vast subject. (*Ash-Shifa'* of *Qadi* 'Iyad: 1.3.1).

Allah confirms in the Qur'an itself that He is its Author, and that neither its contents nor the one to whom it was revealed, may Allah bless him and grant him peace, can be doubted:

In the Name of the Merciful the Compassionate

Blessed is the One Who has revealed the Discrimination (between right and wrong) to His slave (Muhammad), so that he might be a warner to all the worlds – the One to Whom the dominion of the heavens and the earth belongs – and He has not chosen a son, and He does not have any partner to share the dominion, and He has created everything and determined its destiny.

And yet they have chosen gods instead of Him who cannot create anything but are themselves created, and who do not have any power either to harm or to benefit themselves, and who do not have any power over either death or life or raising the dead!

And those who reject say, 'Surely this is nothing but a lie which he has made up with the help of other people – and they have indeed produced misguidance and falsehood!'

And they say, 'Ancient stories which are dictated to him early in the morning and late at night, which he writes down!'

Say: 'It has been revealed by the One Who knows the secret of the heavens and the earth – surely He is always Forgiving, Compassionate.'

And they say, 'What is it with this Messenger, that he eats food, and walks in the market places? Why has an angel not been sent down to him, to be a warner with him? Or why is he not showered with treasure, or given a garden from which to eat?'

And the wrong doers say, 'Surely you are only following a man who has been bewitched!' See what comparisons they make with you, when they are astray and cannot find their way!

Blessed is the One Who if He wishes will give you better than that – Gardens underneath which rivers flow – in which He will give you palaces.

Indeed, they deny the Hour – and for whoever denies the Hour, We have prepared a burning Fire. (25.1-11).

And:

> And I most certainly swear by the movements of the stars – and surely that is a tremendous oath if you only knew – that this is certainly a noble Qur'an, from a closely guarded Book, which cannot be touched except by those who are purified – a revelation from the Lord of the worlds. (56.75-80).

And:

> Will they not reflect on the Qur'an? If it had come from other than Allah, they would certainly have found many inconsistencies in it. (4.82).

And:

> And what about those who disbelieve in the Reminder when it comes to them? Surely it is certainly a mighty Book – falsehood cannot come near it, either from in front of it, or from behind it – a revelation from the Wise, the Worthy of Praise. It does not say anything to you (O Muhammad) other than what has already been said to the Messengers before you – surely your Lord is the Lord of forgiveness, and the Lord of painful punishment. (41.41-43).

Allah also confirms *sayyedina* Muhammad's complete helplessness and dependence on his Lord:

> Say (O Muhammad): 'I am not any different from the (other) Messengers, and I do not know what will be done either with me or with you – I only follow what is inspired in me, and I am only a clear warner.' (46.9).

And:

> Say (O Muhammad): 'I do not say to you that I have the treasures of Allah, or that I know the Unseen – and I do not say to you that I am an angel – surely I only follow what is inspired in me.'
>
> Say: 'Are the blind man and the one who sees clearly equal? Will you not reflect?' (6.50).

And:

> Say (O Muhammad): 'Surely I only pray to my Lord, and I do not associate any partner with Him.'
>
> Say: 'Surely I do not have any power either to harm you or to guide you aright.'
>
> Say: 'Surely no one can protect me from Allah, and I cannot find any refuge instead of Him. I can only convey (what I am told) from Allah, and His messages – and as for whoever disobeys Allah and His Messenger, then surely the Fire of Jahannam is for him, in which he will dwell for ever – until (the Day comes) when they see what they were promised, and then they will know whose helpers are weaker, and whose numbers are less.'
>
> Say: 'I do not know whether what you have been promised is near, or whether my Lord has chosen a time far in the future for it. He knows the Unseen, and He does not reveal what is in the Unseen to anyone – except to the Messengers with whom He is pleased – and then He makes watchers go in front of him and behind him, in order to know whether he has indeed conveyed the messages of their Lord; and He encompasses wherever they are, and He keeps account of everything. (72.20-28).

And:

> And it is not for any person for Allah to speak to him, except by revelation, or from behind a veil, or by sending a Messenger to reveal whatever He wishes by His permission – surely He is Exalted, Wise.
>
> And that is how We have inspired you (O Muhammad) with a spirit by Our command. You did not know about the Book, or about *iman*, but We have made it a light whereby We guide whomever We wish from among Our slaves – and surely you certainly guide to the straight path, the path of Allah – the One to Whom whatever is in the heavens and whatever is in the earth belong.
>
> Does not every thing come back to Allah in the end?
>
> (42.51-53).

One aspect of the miraculous nature of the Qur'an is its clarity and purity of expression and its eloquence. It was revealed at a time when the poetry of the Arabs was at its peak, and yet no one had ever come across anything like it, and no one was able to compose anything like it – a challenge which, as we have already seen, the Qur'an itself makes:

> Say: 'Surely even if all mankind and all the *jinn* combined together to make up something like this Qur'an, they could not produce anything like it, even if they helped each other.
>
> (17.88).

And:

> And this Qur'an could never have been made up by anyone other than Allah – but it is a confirmation of what was (revealed) before it, and an explanation of the Book, in which there is no doubt, from the Lord of the worlds.
>
> Or do they say he has made it up?
>
> Say: 'Then make up a *surah* like it – and call on whomever you can other than Allah (to help you) – if you are speaking the truth.' (10.37-38).

And:

> Or they say, 'He has made it up.'
>
> Say: 'Then bring ten *surahs* like it, which you have made up – and call on whomever you can other than Allah (to help you) – if you are speaking the truth.'
>
> And if they cannot meet your challenge, then know that it has only been revealed by the knowledge of Allah – and that there is no god except Him.
>
> So will you not be Muslims? (11.13-14).

And:

> And if you are in any doubt about what We have revealed to Our slave (Muhammad), then make up a *surah* like it – and call your witnesses instead of Allah if you are speaking the truth.

> And if you cannot do it – and you will never do it – then beware of a Fire whose fuel is men and stones, which has been prepared for those who disbelieve. (2.23-24).

No-one has yet been able to meet this challenge – which has now been in existence for over fourteen centuries – and no one ever will! Qadi 'Iyad states:

> The Qur'an came through the Prophet and he brought it – this is definitely known. It is also known that the Prophet made it a challenge and the Arabs were unable to respond to it. It is known without doubt by those who know eloquence and the techniques of rhetoric that its eloquence is a miracle. The way that someone who is not one of the people of this art knows that it is a miracle is by the incapacity of the skilled people of that art to respond to its challenge and the fact that they have confirmed the inimitability of its eloquence. (*Ash-Shifa'* of *Qadi* 'Iyad: 1.4.4).

It should be noted in passing that *sayyedina* Muhammad, may Allah bless him and grant him peace, was given companions not only amongst humans, but also amongst the *jinn*, as Allah confirms more than once in the Qur'an:

> **And (remember) when We directed a group of the *jinn* to you (O Muhammad) to listen to the Qur'an – and when they were in its presence, they said (to each other), 'Be quiet!' – and when it was finished they returned to warn their people, saying, 'O our people, surely we have been listening to a Book which has been revealed after Musa, confirming what came before it and guiding to the truth and to the straight way. O our people, respond to the one who calls to Allah and trust in Him – He will forgive you your wrong actions and protect you from a painful punishment.'**
>
> **And as for whoever does not respond to the one who calls to Allah, there is no escape in the earth and no one instead of Him to protect him – these are clearly astray. (46.29-32).**

And:

> **In the Name of Allah the Merciful the Compassionate**

> Say: 'It has been revealed to me that a group of the *jinn* listened (to the Qur'an), and they said, "Surely we have heard a wonderful Qur'an which guides to what is right, so we have believed in it – and we will never associate any partner with our Lord; and that He – may the Majesty of our Lord be exalted – has not taken either a wife or a son; and that the foolish among us used to tell lies about Allah – and we thought that neither mankind nor the *jinn* would ever utter a lie about Allah; and that there used to be people from among mankind who sought the protection of people from among the *jinn*, thereby increasing their misfortune – and they certainly used to think, just as you think, that Allah would never bring anyone back to life (on the Last Day); and that we used to search in the heaven, but we found it filled with powerful guards and shooting stars; and that we used to sit in places up there, listening – but now whoever tries to listen finds a shooting star waiting for him – and so we do not know whether evil is intended for those on earth, or whether their Lord intends them to go right; and that among us are those who are righteous, and among us are those who are other than that – we have different ways; and that we know that we can never escape Allah on earth and that we can never escape Him in flight; and that when we heard the guidance, we believed in it – and whoever believes in his Lord need not fear any loss or misfortune; and that among us are those who are Muslims, and among us are those who have gone off course – and as for whoever submits (to Allah), then these have taken the right way – and as for those who have gone off course, then they are fuel for *Jahannam*."' (72.1-15).

Another fact which infuriated those who rejected the Prophet Muhammad, may Allah bless him and grant him peace, and who claimed that either he was making the Qur'an up, or that he was possessed by *jinn*, was the fact that his ordinary speech was not only very different to the language of the Qur'an, but also it was far too lucid to be the language of a madman or a man possessed:

> When al-Walid ibn al-Mughira heard the ordinary speech of the Prophet and then the Qur'an was recited to him, he softened and Abu Jahl went to him to rebuke him. He said, 'By

Allah, there is none of you who knows poetry better than I, and by Allah, his ordinary speech does not resemble this (the Qur'an) in any way.'

Another tradition reports the Quraysh gathering together at the time of their annual fair and saying, 'The delegations of the Arabs are coming, so let us agree on one opinion about him so that we will not contradict each other.' They said, 'We say he is a soothsayer.' Al-Walid said, 'By Allah, he is not a soothsayer. He does not mutter nor speak in rhymed prose.' They said, 'He is mad, possessed by a *jinn*.' He said, 'He is not mad nor *jinn*-possessed. There is no choking nor whispering.' They said, 'We say he is a poet.' He said, 'He is not a poet. We know poetry in all its forms and metres and he is not a poet.' They said, 'We say he is a sorcerer.' He said, 'He is not a sorcerer – there is no spitting and no knots.' They said, 'Then what will we say?'

He said, 'You have not said anything about this matter which I do not recognise to be false. The closest you have come is the statement that he is a sorcerer, for magic is something that can come between a man and his son, a man and his brother, a man and his wife, and a man and his tribe.' Then they separated and sat down in the road to warn people. Allah revealed about al-Walid, **'Leave Me and the one I created alone.' (74.11)**. (Al-Bayhaqi).

When 'Utba ibn Rabi'a heard the Qur'an, he said, 'O people! You know that I have not left anything without learning it, reading it and saying it. By Allah, I have heard a type of speech, and by Allah, I have never heard anything like it. It (the Qur'an) is not poetry and it is not spells nor soothsaying.' An-Nadr ibn al-Harith said something similar.

In the *hadith* of Abu Dharr becoming Muslim, he describes his brother Unays and says, 'By Allah, I have not heard of anyone who knows more poetry than my brother Unays. He contested with twelve poets in the *Jahiliyya* and I was one of them.' This brother went to Makka and on his return told Abu Dharr about the Prophet. Abu Dharr asked, 'What do people say?' He replied, 'They say he is a poet, a soothsayer and a sorcerer. I have heard the words of the soothsayers and this is not like their words. I compared him with the reciters of poetry and it was not like them. No one after me should err and say he was a poet. He is truthful and they are liars. (Muslim). (*Ash-Shifa'* of Qadi 'Iyad: 1.4.5).

The Qur'an not only contains descriptions of the Creator and the created – descriptions of how the universe came into being and of how it is sustained, both in the Seen and in the Unseen worlds – but also, as we have already repeatedly seen in all three volumes of *Prophets in the Qur'an*, it contains accounts of events that had already taken place in the past which the Prophet Muhammad could not possibly have known or found out about by himself, may Allah bless him and grant him peace, until they were revealed. *Qadi* 'Iyad states:

> The Prophet brought these reports in the proper way with proper texts, so that all men of knowledge were forced to admit their soundness and truthfulness and that they could not have been gained through study. They knew that the Prophet was illiterate and could not read or write and was not occupied with study or constant research. He did not travel away from his people and people were not unaware of his situation.
>
> The People of the Book used to question him a lot about these things, so he recited to them the part of the Qur'an that was revealed to him which dealt with such things as the accounts of the Prophets' dealings with their peoples, the story of Musa and al-Khidr, Yusuf and his brothers, the people of the Cave, Dhu'l-Qarnayn, Luqman and his son, and other similar reports about the various Prophets, and the account of the beginning of creation and what was in the Torah and the Injil (Evangel) and the Zabur (Psalms) and the Scrolls of Ibrahim and Musa.
>
> The men of knowledge confirmed him in this, not being able to deny it but rather affirming it. Those who were destined to ultimate success in the Hereafter believed in the good that came to him, while those whose lot in the Hereafter was wretchedness remained stubborn and envious.
>
> Furthermore, there is no evidence of denial of these things on the part of any of the Christians or the Jews, in spite of their intense enmity towards the Prophet and the fact that they urged people to deny him and argued against him by what was in their books and rebuked him by what their books contained.
>
> They did not deny what had come in the Qur'an despite the abundance of their questions to him and the fact that they pressured him with difficult questions about their Prophets, the secrets of their knowledges, the contents of their biographies and information about what was hidden inside their *shari'as* and the contents of their books – like their asking about the Spirit, Dhu'l-

Qarnayn, the People of the Cave, 'Isa, the judgement of the strong and what Isra'il (Ya'qub) made *haram* for himself and what had become *haram* for them of beasts and good things which had previously been lawful for them and was then made forbidden for them because of their outrageous behaviour.

Allah says, **'That is their likeness in the Torah and their likeness in the Injil.'** (48.29).

Other such matters were revealed in the Qur'an, and he answered them and acquainted them with what had been revealed to him about them. It is not known that any of them rejected or denied any of this. Most of them declared the validity of his prophecy and the truthfulness of what he said and admitted their stubbornness and envy of the Prophet – like the people of Najran (the community of Christians who argued with him about *sayyedina* 'Isa, peace be on him), and Ibn Suriya (the Jewish rabbi in Madina who tried to cover up the verse of stoning in the Taurah), and the sons of Akhtab (Huyayy and Abu Yasir, the father and uncle of Safiyyah, one of the wives of the Prophet Muhammad), and others. (*Ash-Shifa'* of *Qadi* 'Iyad: 1.4.7).

As well as dealing with the past, the Qur'an also deals with the present: Certain *ayat* in the Qur'an were initially revealed as a specific guidance to be followed by the Prophet Muhammad and his companions in the particular situations which existed at the time that they were revealed. As well as providing specific guidance at that time, these *ayat* have continued ever since to indicate what should be done when Muslims find themselves in similar situations – for although outward appearances have always been changing, the human condition has always remained essentially the same.

This is why it is often so important to know the context in which particular *ayat* were originally revealed so that they can be both fully understood and correctly applied, without any danger of misinterpretation or misapplication. Thus it is necessary to have a sound knowledge of the history of the lives of the Prophet Muhammad and his companions, may the blessings and peace of Allah be on him and them, in order to fully appreciate the significance and meaning of particular passages in the Qur'an – which continue to have as much relevance today as they did when first revealed.

As well as dealing with the present, the Qur'an also contains predictions about the future, some of which were fulfilled during *sayyedina* Muhammad's lifetime – such as the conquest of Makka by the Muslims, for example; and some of which were fulfilled after his death – such as the defeat of the Persians by the Greeks, for example; and some of which still remain to be fulfilled – such as, for example, the end of the world and the coming of the Last Day.

Thus as well as dealing with this world and defining what behaviour is necessary, or acceptable, or unacceptable, or forbidden, the Qur'an also describes the consequences of these different kinds of behaviour, not only in this world, but also in the next world which is described in precise detail, both its Garden and its Fire – and there is no other alternative.

It has been related by at-Tirmidhi that the Prophet Muhammad, may Allah bless him and grant him peace, said, 'Allah sent down this Qur'an to command and prevent, and as a *sunna* to be followed and a parable. It contains your history, information about what came before you, news about what will come after you and correct judgement between you. Repetition does not wear it out and its wonders do not end. It is the Truth. It is not a jest. Whoever recites it speaks the truth. Whoever judges by it is just. Whoever argues by it wins. Whoever divides by it is equitable. Whoever acts by it is rewarded. Whoever clings to it is guided to a straight path. Allah will misguide whoever seeks guidance from other than it. Allah will destroy whoever judges by other than it. It is the Wise Remembrance, the Clear Light, the Straight Path, the Firm Rope of Allah and the Useful Healing. It is a protection for the one who clings to it and a rescue for the one who follows it. It is not crooked and so puts things straight. It does not deviate so as to be blamed. Its wonders do not cease. It does not wear out with much repetition.'

As well as confirming from Whom and to whom the Qur'an was revealed, Allah also confirms by whom it was revealed:

> **Say (O Muhammad): 'Who is an enemy to Jibril?' – for surely it is he who has revealed it (the Qur'an) to your heart by the permission of Allah, confirming what was (revealed) before it, and a guidance and good news to the believers. – 'Who is an enemy to Allah, and to His angels, and to His Messengers, and to Jibril, and to Mika'il? –Then surely Allah is an enemy to those who reject.' (2.97-98).**

And:

> Say: 'The holy spirit (Jibril) has revealed it from your Lord with truth – so that it may strengthen those who believe – as a guidance and good news for those who are Muslims.
>
> (16.102).

Allah clearly states what the Qur'an is not as well as what it is:

> And I most certainly swear – by what you see, and by what you do not see – that it (the Qur'an) is indeed expressed by a noble Messenger (Jibril).
>
> And it is not the speech of a poet – how little you believe! And it is not the speech of a soothsayer – how little you remember!
>
> It is a revelation from the Lord of the worlds.
>
> And if he (Muhammad) had said anything untrue about Us, We would certainly have seized him by the right hand and then We would certainly have severed his life-artery – and not one of you would have been able to restrain Us from him!
>
> And surely it is certainly a reminder for those who have *taqwa*.
>
> And surely We certainly know that some of you will deny it – and surely it will certainly distress the disbelievers.
>
> And surely it is certainly the absolute truth – so glorify the Name of your Tremendous Lord. (69.38-52).

And:

> And I most certainly swear by the planets – by the stars that rise and set, and by the night when it comes to an end, and by the morning when it comes to life – that it (the Qur'an) is indeed expressed by a noble Messenger (Jibril) who is established in power from the Lord of the Throne – to be obeyed and also trusted.
>
> And your companion (Muhammad) is not mad; and he certainly saw him (Jibril) on the clear horizon – and he is not

eager to know the Unseen; and it (the Qur'an) is not the speech of an outcast *shaytan*.

So, where are *you* going?

Surely it is nothing but a reminder to all the worlds, for whomever of you who wants to go straight; and you will not want it unless Allah wants it – the Lord of the worlds.

(81.15-29).

As well as saying who it is from, Allah also clearly says who the Qur'an is for:

In the Name of Allah the Merciful the Compassionate

Alif   Lam   Mim

That is the Book in which there is no doubt, a guidance for those who have *taqwa* – those who believe in the Unseen, and who establish the prayer, and who spend out of what We have given them, and those who believe in what is revealed to you (Muhammad), and in what was revealed before you, and who are certain about the next world – these are following guidance from their Lord, and these are the ones who are successful. (2.1-10).

And:

And what about the one whose heart Allah has expanded to Islam so that he follows a light from his Lord? And woe to those whose hearts are hardened against the remembrance of Allah – these are clearly astray.

Allah has revealed the best of what can be said, a Book which is consistent in what it says, which makes the skin of those who fear their Lord tingle, so that their skin and their hearts soften to the remembrance of Allah – that is Allah's guidance, whereby He guides whomever He wishes – and as for whomever Allah leads astray, there is no guide for him. (39.22-23).

One of the wives of *sayyedina* Muhammad – 'A'isha, may Allah be pleased with her – was once asked what the Prophet Muhammad was like. She replied, 'The Qur'an walking,' indicating that he fully embodied the teaching that had been revealed to him. Thus whoever would like to understand the Messenger should read the message that he was given – the Qur'an – and whoever would like to understand the message should learn how *sayyedina* Muhammad behaved and try to behave likewise. Allah says in the Qur'an:

> **Certainly there is a good example in the Messenger of Allah for you – for whoever regards Allah and the Last Day with hope and remembers Allah a great deal. (33.21).**

And:

> **And surely you (O Muhammad) have a tremendous nature.**
> **(68.4).**

Indeed it was necessary for the Prophet Muhammad to have such a tremendous nature, may Allah bless him and grant him peace, in order for him to be able to bear the tremendous power of the Qur'an, of which Allah says:

> **If We had revealed this Qur'an to a mountain, you would certainly have seen it brought low, splitting apart out of fear of Allah – and such are the comparisons which We make for people so that perhaps they may reflect. (59.21).**

It has been transmitted by 'A'isha, may Allah be pleased with her, that al-Harith ibn Hisham asked the Prophet Muhammad, may Allah bless him and grant him peace, 'How does the revelation come to you?' and he replied, 'Sometimes it comes to me like the ringing of a bell, and that is the hardest for me, and when it leaves me I remember what it has said. And sometimes the angel (Jibril) appears to me in the likeness of a man and talks to me and I remember what he says.' 'A'isha added, 'I saw it coming down on him on an intensely cold day, and when it had left him his forehead was dripping with sweat.' (*Al-Muwatta'* of *Imam* Malik: 15.4.7).

It has been related by 'Ubada ibn Samit that when the revelation descended on *sayyedina* Muhammad, may Allah bless him and grant him peace, he would lower his head, and so his Companions would lower their heads, may Allah be pleased with them, and then when it was over, he would raise his head. (Muslim).

Although *sayyedina* Muhammad, may Allah bless him and grant him peace, is not directly referred to by name very often in the Qur'an, there are many *ayat* in which he is addressed directly as 'O Prophet' and 'O Messenger' and often, as we have already seen, simply as 'you' – it being clear from the context that the *ayat* are directed to *sayyedina* Muhammad, may Allah bless him and grant him peace – as, for example, in Surah Ya Sin:

> **In the Name of Allah the Merciful the Compassionate**
>
> **Ya Sin**
>
> **By the wise Qur'an, surely you are one of those who have been sent, on a straight path, with a revelation from the Mighty, the Compassionate, so that you may warn a people whose fathers were not warned – and so they are heedless.**
>
> (36.1-6).

And:

> **In the Name of Allah the Merciful the Compassionate**
>
> **Alif Lam Mim**
>
> **Allah – there is no god except Him, the Living, the Eternal**
>
> **He has revealed the Book to you with the truth, confirming what was (revealed) before it, just as He revealed the Taurah and the Injil. (3.1-4).**

It would be interesting to consider in passing what *Qadi* 'Iyad says about the letters which appear at the beginning of the *surahs* which have been quoted above – and whose meaning and significance are sometimes misunderstood or misinterpreted:

> Allah says, **'Ya Sin. By the Wise Qur'an.'** (36.1-2). The commentators disagree about the meaning of *Ya Sin*, saying different things about it. Abu Muhammad Makki related that the Prophet said, 'I have ten names with my Lord.' He mentioned *Ta Ha* and *Ya Sin* as two of these names. Abu 'Abdu'r-Rahman as-Sulami related that Ja'far as-Sadiq said that the meaning of *Ya Sin* is, 'O master!' (*Ya Sayyid*) addressing the Prophet. Ibn 'Abbas said that *Ya Sin* means 'O man' (*Ya Insan*), i.e. Muhammad. He also said that it is an oath and one of the Names

of Allah. Az-Zajjaj said that it means, 'O Muhammad'. It is said that it means, 'O man' or 'O human'. Ibn al-Hanafiyyah said that *Ya Sin* means 'O Muhammad'.

Ka'b said that *Ya Sin* is an oath by which Allah swore a thousand years before He created heaven and earth, meaning, 'O Muhammad, you are one of the Messengers.'

Then Allah continues, ' **By the Wise Qur'an, you are truly one of the Messengers.'** (36.2-3). If it is confirmed that *Ya Sin* is one of the names of the Prophet, and it is a valid oath, then it certainly involves respect, and the first oath is further strengthened by being joined to the second oath. Although it is in the vocative case, Allah invokes another oath after it to verify the Prophet's messengership and to attest to the truth of his guidance. Allah swears by the Prophet's name and His Book that he is one of the Messengers bearing His revelation to His slaves and that he is on a straight path by his belief, i.e. a path without any crookedness or deviation from the truth.

An-Naqqash said, 'In His Book, Allah did not swear by any of His Prophets that they were Messengers except for Muhammad.'

In the case of those who interpret it as meaning, 'O master', the use of *Ya Sin* definitely shows Allah's high esteem for him. And indeed the Prophet himself said, 'I am the master of the children of Adam, and it is no boast.' (Muslim and at-Tirmidhi). (*Ash-Shifa'* of *Qadi* 'Iyad: 1.1.4).

And:

Allah says, **'Alif Lam Mim. That Book. No doubt in it.'** (2.1-2). Ibn 'Abbas said that these letters are oaths by which Allah swears. He and other people have said various things about them.

Sahl at-Tustari said, 'The *Alif* is Allah, the *Lam* is Jibril, and the *Mim* is Muhammad, may Allah bless him and grant him peace.' As-Samarqandi also said this, but did not attribute it to Sahl. He said that it means that Allah sent down Jibril to Muhammad with this Book in which there is no doubt. According to the first interpretation, the import of the oath is that this Book is true without doubt and it involves the direct connection of the two names – a matter whose excellence has previously been stated. (*Ash-Shifa'* of *Qadi* 'Iyad: 1.1.4).

The meaning and purpose of the Prophet Muhammad, may Allah bless him and grant him peace, is confirmed again and again in the Qur'an – as, for example, in Surat al-Furqan:

> And We have only sent you (O Muhammad) as a bringer of good news, and as a warner.
>
> Say: 'I do not ask you for any payment for this – except that whoever wants it should choose a way to his Lord.'
> (25.56-57).

And in Surah Saba:

> And We have sent you (O Muhammad) only as a bringer of good news, and as a warner, to all of mankind – but most people do not know.
>
> And they say, 'When will this promise (be fulfilled) if you are speaking the truth?'
>
> Say: 'You have been promised a Day which you cannot move back or bring forward an hour.' (34.28-30).

And in Surat al-Ahzab:

> O Prophet, surely We have sent you as a witness, and as a bringer of good news, and as a warner, and as one who calls to Allah by His permission, and as a light giving lamp.
> (33.45-46).

Allah describes the nature of light in Surat an-Nur:

> Allah is the One Who illuminates the heavens and the earth. The likeness of His light is as if there were a niche and in the niche is a lamp and in the lamp is a glass and the glass as it were a brilliant star, lit from a blessed tree, an olive, neither of the east nor of the west, whose oil is well nigh luminous, though fire has scarce touched it, Light upon Light. Allah guides the ones He wants to His light, and Allah strikes metaphors for mankind, and Allah is aware of everything. (24.35).

This *ayah* has many meanings, and one of them is that the niche is the universe, and the lamp is *sayyedina* Muhammad, may Allah bless him and grant him peace, and the glass which is like a brilliant star is his heart and what it contains, and Allah knows best.

As we have already seen in *Volume Two*, Allah says:

> O People of the Book, now has Our Messenger indeed come to you, making clear to you much of what you used to hide in the Book, and forgiving much.
>
> Now there has indeed come to you from Allah a Light and a clear Book, whereby Allah guides whoever seeks His pleasure to paths of peace – and He brings them out of darkness into light by His decree, and guides them to a straight path.
>
> (5.15-16).

And:

> In the Name of Allah the Merciful the Compassionate
>
> Those who disbelieve from among the People of the Book and those who worship idols could not have ceased (doing so) until clear proof came to them:
>
> A Messenger from Allah, reciting from a Book free from impurity containing true revelations.
>
> And the People who were given the Book did not become divided until after clear proof came to them, and they were not commanded (to do) anything other than to worship Allah, sincere to Him in their *deen* – *hanif* – and to establish the prayer and to pay the *zakat* – and that is the true *deen*.
>
> Surely those who disbelieve from among the People of the Book and those who worship idols will abide in the Fire of Hell for ever. They are the worst of created beings.
>
> Surely those who trust and do good are the best of created beings. Their reward is with their Lord – Gardens of Eden underneath which rivers flow, in which they will dwell for ever. Allah is pleased with them and they are pleased with Him. – This is for whoever fears his Lord. (98.1-8).

Allah also says:

> He is the One Who has sent His Messenger with guidance

and the true *deen* so that He may make it overcome all other religions – and Allah is enough as a Witness.

Muhammad is the Messenger of Allah, and those who are with him are harsh with the disbelievers and merciful with each other – you see them bowing and prostrating, seeking the generosity of Allah and His pleasure – their mark is on their faces, from the traces of prostrating – that is their likeness in the Taurah and their likeness in the Ingil – like a seed which is planted, producing a shoot and then making it grow stronger, rising up on its stalk, to the delight of those who planted it – so that He makes the disbelievers furious at them.

Allah has promised those among them who believe and do good, forgiveness and a tremendous reward. (48.28-29).

And:

And the believing men and the believing women are a protection for each other – they command what is good, and they forbid what is bad, and they establish the prayer, and they pay the *zakat*, and they obey Allah and His Messenger – these are the ones on whom Allah will have mercy – surely Allah is Mighty, Wise.

Allah has promised the believing men and the believing women Gardens underneath which rivers flow in which they will live for ever, in pleasant dwellings in the Garden of Eden – and, which is better, acceptance from Allah – that is indeed the supreme success.

O Prophet, fight the disbelievers and the hypocrites and be harsh with them – their dwelling place will be Jahannam – what an awful journey's end! (9.71-73).

And:

In the Name of Allah the Merciful the Compassionate

As for those who disbelieve and turn people away from the way of Allah, He makes their actions go astray, and as for those who believe and do good and believe in what has been revealed to Muhammad – and it (the Qur'an) is the truth from their Lord – He cancels out their sins and puts their hearts right. That is because those who disbelieve follow what is false, and those who believe follow the truth from their Lord – that is how Allah strikes meta-phors for mankind. (47.1-3).

And:

Muhammad is not the father of any man among you, but he is the Messenger of Allah, and the Seal of the Prophets – and Allah is always aware of everything.

O you who believe, remember Allah with a great deal of remembrance, and glorify Him in the early morning and in the evening.

He is the One who blesses you – and His angels – so that He may bring you out of darkness into light; and He is always Compassionate with the believers.

Their greeting on the Day that they meet Him will be, 'Peace'; and He has prepared a generous reward for them.

(33.40-44).

And:

O you who believe, bow down, and prostrate, and worship your Lord, and do good, so that you may be successful – and strive for Allah with the striving which is due to Him.

He has chosen you and He has not imposed anything difficult on you in the *deen* – the way of your forefather Ibrahim. He has described you as Muslims, both in the past and in this (Qur'an), so that the Messenger (Muhammad) may be a witness for you, and so that you may be witnesses for mankind; so establish the prayer and pay the *zakat* and hold firmly to Allah – He is your Protector, a blessed Protector and a blessed Helper. (22.77-78).

And:

Surely We have sent you (O Muhammad) as a witness, and as a bringer of good news, and as a warner – so that you (O mankind) may believe in Allah and in His Messenger, and honour Him, and revere Him, and glorify Him early in the morning and in the evening.

> Surely those who swear allegiance to you (O Muhammad) are in fact swearing allegiance to Allah – the hand of Allah is over their hands.
>
> And as for whoever breaks his oath, then he only breaks it to his own loss – and as for whoever fulfils his covenant with Allah, then He will grant him a tremendous reward.
>
> (48.8-10).

It is for this reason that Allah says:

> Whoever obeys the Messenger has certainly obeyed Allah – and as for whoever turns away, We have not sent you (Muhammad) to keep watch over them. (4.80).

And:

> Say (O Muhammad): 'If you love Allah, then follow me, and Allah will love you and forgive you your wrong actions,' – and Allah is Forgiving, Compassionate.
>
> Say: 'Obey Allah and the Messenger – and if they turn away, then surely Allah does not love the disbelievers. (3.31-32).

When considering the above *ayat*, Qadi 'Iyad states:

> It is related that 'Umar, may Allah be pleased with him, said to the Prophet, 'Part of your excellence with Allah is that He has made obedience to you obedience to Him. Allah says, **'Whoever obeys the Messenger has obeyed Allah,'** (4.80) and, **'If you love Allah, then follow me and Allah will love you.'"** (3.31). It is related that when this *ayah* was sent down, people said, 'Muhammad wants us to take him as a mercy in the way the Christians did with 'Isa,' so Allah revealed, **'Say: "Obey Allah and the Messenger ,"'** (3.32). (Ibn al-Jawzi). Allah connected obedience to Muhammad with obedience to Himself in spite of what the people said. (*Ash-Shifa'* of *Qadi* 'Iyad: 1.1.1).

It has been transmitted by 'Umar, may Allah be pleased with him, that he heard the Prophet Muhammad, may Allah bless him and grant him peace, say, 'Do not praise me as the Christians have praised the son of Mary, for surely I am only a slave – so call me 'the slave of Allah and His Messenger'. (Al-Bukhari).

The Qur'an repeatedly emphasises the reason why people should obey Allah and His Messenger, may Allah bless him and grant him peace – it is not for Allah's benefit, but for their *own* benefit:

> And obey Allah and the Messenger so that you may be treated with mercy – and compete with each other for forgiveness from your Lord, and for a Garden as wide as the heavens and the earth which has been prepared for those who have *taqwa* – those who spend (on others) in times of ease and hardship, and who control their anger, and who are forgiving towards people – and Allah loves those who are good; and those who, when they do something bad or wrong themselves, remember Allah and ask for forgiveness for their wrong actions – and who can forgive wrong actions except Allah? – and do not intentionally persist in what they were doing.
>
> The reward of these will be forgiveness from their Lord, and Gardens underneath which rivers flow, in which they will dwell for ever – what a blessed reward for those who tried hard! (3.132-136).

And:

> O you who believe, respond to Allah and to the Messenger when you are called to what will bring you to life – and know that Allah comes between a man and his heart, and that it is to Him that you will be gathered.
>
> And beware of affliction which will not only strike those who do wrong in particular – and know that Allah is severe in punishment.
>
> And remember when there were only a few of you, and you were considered weak in the land, and you were afraid that people might overcome you – and how He gave you refuge, and strengthened you with His help, and provided you with good things so that you would be grateful.
>
> O you who believe, do not betray Allah and the Messenger, and do not intentionally betray what has been entrusted

to you – and know that surely your possessions and your children are a test, and that it is with Allah that there is a tremendous reward.

O you who believe, if you have *taqwa* of Allah, then He will give you discrimination (between good and bad), and He will free you from your sins, and He will forgive you – and Allah possesses tremendous generosity. (8.24-29).

It is because obedience to the Prophet Muhammad *is* obedience to Allah that Allah has always made those who obey Allah and His Messenger extremely close to *sayyedina* Muhammad, may Allah bless him and grant him peace, and to each other:

The Prophet is closer to the believers than their own selves; and his wives are (as) their mothers; and those who are related by kinship are closer to each other in the Book of Allah than the (other) believers and the *Muhajirun* – although you should be kind to your friends. That has always been written in the Book. (33.6).

(It should be noted that as well as emphasising the closeness between *sayyedina* Muhammad and those who follow him, this *ayah* also makes it clear that in spite of this closeness, those who inherit from a dead believer's wealth do so by virtue of kinship, and not simply because of their shared faith.)

Allah also addressed the Prophet Muhammad, may Allah bless him and grant him peace, with these words:

And if they (the disbelievers) want to trick you, then surely Allah is enough for you: He is the One Who has supported you with His help – and with the believers – and He has brought their hearts together. If you had expended all that is in the earth, you could not have brought their hearts together, but Allah brought them together – surely He is the Mighty, the Wise.

O Prophet, Allah is enough for you, and for whomever of the believers who follow you. (8.63-64).

It is clear that the above *ayat* refer principally to those who followed *sayyedina* Muhammad during his lifetime, of whom Allah also says:

> You are the best community that has been raised up for mankind, commanding what is good and forbidding what is bad and believing in Allah.
>
> And if only the People of the Book had believed, it would certainly have been better for them. Some of them are believers, but most of them are evil livers. (3.110).

It is, however, equally clear that the above three passages also refer to the believers in *every* age, both before and after *sayyedina* Muhammad, may the blessings and peace of Allah be on him and them, and it is for this reason that Allah refers to those who obey Allah and the Prophet Muhammad as being in the best of company:

> And as for whoever obeys Allah and the Messenger, they are with those whom Allah has blessed – the Prophets, and those who speak the truth, and the martyrs, and the righteous – and they are the best company! (4.69).

And these *are* the blessed people – the people whom Allah has blessed – to whom Allah refers in Surat al-Fatiha:

> Lead us on the straight path, the path of those whom You have blessed – not of those with whom You are angry, and not of those who are astray. (1.6-7).

It is generally agreed among the commentators on the Qur'an that one of the meanings of these *ayat* is that **'those whom You have blessed'** refers to those who obey Allah and His Messenger, may Allah bless him and grant him peace, that **'those with whom You are angry'** refers to the Jews, and that **'those who are astray'** refers to the Christians, and Allah knows best. Qadi 'Iyad states:

> The commentators disagree about the meaning of the words of Allah in the *Fatiha*, **'Guide us on the Straight Path, the path of those You have blessed.'** Abu'l-'Aliyya and al-Hasan al-Basri said, 'The Straight Path is the Messenger of Allah and the best of the people of his House and his Companions.'
>
> Makki related something similar, 'This refers to the Messenger of Allah, may Allah bless him and grant him peace, and his two Companions, Abu Bakr and 'Umar, may Allah be pleased with them both.'

Abu'l-Layth as-Samarqandi related almost the same from Abu'l-'Aliyya regarding the words of Allah, **'the path of those You have blessed.'** Al-Hasan al-Basri heard it and said, 'It is true, by Allah, and it is good counsel.' (*Ash-Shifa'* of Qadi 'Iyad: 1.1.1).

It is for this reason that those who strive to obey Allah have always sought knowledge of Allah and His Messenger, may Allah bless him and grant him peace, and this is why Allah says:

O you who believe, have *taqwa* of Allah and be with the truthful ones. (9.119).

One of the signs of the truthful ones is not only their profound knowledge but also their deep love for Allah and His Messenger, may Allah bless him and grant him peace. As the following passages from *Ash-Shifa'* of Qadi 'Iyad indicate, this great love and respect for *sayyedina* Muhammad was not only experienced by his companions, but has also been experienced by those have followed in the dust of their footsteps ever since:

'Amr ibn al-'As said, 'There is no one I have loved more than the Messenger of Allah nor anyone I have respected more. I could never get my fill of looking at him due to my great respect for him. If I had been asked to describe him, I could not have done so because I was unable to look at him enough.'

At-Tirmidhi related that Anas said, 'The Messenger of Allah used to go out with his Companions from the *Muhajirun* and *Ansar* when Abu Bakr and 'Umar were with them. None of them raised their eyes to look at him except Abu Bakr and 'Umar. They would look at him and he at them. They would smile at him and he at them.'

It is related that Usama ibn Sharik said, 'I came to the Prophet and found his Companions sitting around him as still as if there were birds on their heads. (At-Tirmidhi).

In a *hadith* describing him from Hind bint Abi Hala we find, 'When he spoke, those sitting around him bowed their heads as if there were birds on top of them.'

When Quraysh sent 'Urwa ibn Mas'ud to the Messenger of Allah in the year of al-Hudaybiyya (6 AH), he saw the unparalleled respect which his Companions displayed towards him. Whenever he did *wudu'* they ran to get his leftover *wudu'* water and very nearly fought over it. If he spat they took it with their hands and wiped it on their faces and bodies. If a hair of his fell they ran to get it. If he commanded them to do something, they ran to do his command. If he spoke, they lowered their voices in his presence. They did not stare at him due to their respect for him.

When he returned to Quraysh, he said, 'People of Quraysh! I have been to Chosroes in his kingdom, and Caesar in his kingdom and the Negus in his kingdom, but by Allah, I have not seen any king among his people treated anything like the way Muhammad is treated by his Companions.' (Al-Bukh-ari).

One version has, 'I have never seen a king whose companions esteemed him as Muhammad is esteemed by his Companions. I have seen a people who will never abandon him.'

Anas said, 'I saw the Messenger of Allah when his hair was being shaved. His companions were around him and whenever a lock fell, a man picked it up.' (Muslim).

Another instance of this is when Quraysh gave 'Uthman permission to do *tawaf* of the House when the Prophet sent him as an envoy to them and he refused, saying, 'I will not do it until the Messenger of Allah does.'

Talha said that the Companions of the Messenger of Allah told an ignorant bedouin to ask the Prophet about what someone who had fulfilled his vow (to be true to Allah) was like. They were in awe of the Prophet and revered him. He asked him but he did not respond. When Talha came up, the Messenger of Allah said, 'This is someone who has fulfilled his vow.'

Qayla said, 'When I saw the Messenger of Allah sitting squatting, I trembled from fear.' (At-Tirmidhi). This was due to her awe and respect for him.

Al-Mughira said, 'The Companions of the Messenger of Allah would knock on his door with their fingernails.' (Al-Bayhaqi).

Al-Bara' ibn 'Azib said, 'I wanted to ask the Messenger of Allah about something but waited for years out of awe of him.' (Abu Ya'la). (*Ash-Shifa'* of *Qadi* 'Iyad: 2.3.2).

And:

Abu Hurayra said, 'I have not seen anything more beautiful than the Messenger of Allah. It was as if the sun was shining in his face. When he laughed, it reflected from the wall.'

Jabir ibn Samura was asked, 'Was his face like a sword?' He replied, 'No, it was like the sun and the moon. It was round.' (Al-Bukhari and Muslim).

In her description, Umm Ma'bad said, 'From afar, he was the most beautiful of people, and close up he was the most handsome.' (Al-Bayhaqi).

Ibn Abi Hala said, 'His face shone like the full moon.'

At the end of his description, 'Ali said, 'Anyone who saw him suddenly was filled with awe of him. Those who kept his company loved him.'

All who described him said they had not seen anyone like him either before or since. (*Ash-Shifa'* of *Qadi 'Iyad*: 1.2.2).

After describing many of *sayyedina* Muhammad's attributes, may Allah bless him and grant him peace, and the way in which he behaved, *Qadi 'Iyad* concludes:

> We have told you about some of his praiseworthy qualities, glorious virtues and attributes of perfection. We have shown you that he truly had them, and we have presented ample traditions to support this. The matter itself is far more extensive, so although this chapter about him ranges wide, we have hardly even begun to exhaust all the proofs. The ocean of the knowledge of his qualities is overflowing. Bucket-fulls drawn from it have a negligible effect upon it.
>
> However, we think that we should finish these sections with al-Hasan's *hadith* from Ibn Abi Hala since it covers so many of his qualities and includes quite a lot of his biographical detail.
>
> Al-Hasan ibn 'Ali said, 'I asked my uncle Hind ibn Abi Hala about the features of the Messenger of Allah since he was wont to describe them. I wanted him to describe them to me so that I could retain them in my mind.
>
> 'He said, "The Messenger of Allah, may Allah bless him and grant him peace, was imposing and majestic. His face shone like the full moon. He was somewhat taller than medium height and a little shorter than what could be described as tall. His head was large and he had hair that was neither curly nor straight. It was parted, and did not go beyond the lobes of his ears. He was

very fair-skinned with a wide brow, and had thick eye-brows with a narrow space between them. He had a vein there which throbbed when he was angry. He had a long nose with a line of light over it which someone might unthinkingly take to be his nose.

"His beard was thick. He had black eyes, firm cheeks, a wide mouth and white teeth with gaps. The hair of his chest formed a fine line. His neck was like that of a statue made of pure silver.

"His physique was finely-balanced. His body was firm and full. His belly and chest were equal in size. His chest was broad and the space between his shoulders wide. He had full calves. He was luminous.

"Between his neck and his navel there was a line of hair, but the rest of his torso was free of it. He had hair on his forearms and shoulders and the upper part of his chest. He had thick wrists, wide palms, rough hands and feet. His fingers were long. He was fine sinewed. He had high insteps and his feet were so smooth that water ran off them.

"When he walked, he walked as though he were going down a hill. He walked in a dignified manner and walked easily. He walked swiftly. When he walked, it was as though he were heading down a slope. When he turned to address somebody, he turned his whole body completely. He lowered his glance, glancing downwards more than upwards. He restrained his glance. He spoke first to his Companions and was the first to greet any person he met."'

Al-Hasan said, 'Tell me how he spoke.'

Ibn Abi Hala replied, 'The Messenger of Allah, may Allah bless him and grant him peace, was always subject to grief and was always reflective. He had no rest and he only spoke when it was necessary. He spent long periods in silence. He began and ended what he said correctly. His words were comprehensive without being either superfluous or wordy or inadequate.

'He had a mild temperament, being neither harsh nor cruel. He valued a gift, even if it was small. He did not censure anything nor criticise or praise the taste of food. He did not get angry because of it. He did not attend to securing his own due nor did he get angry for himself nor help himself.

'When he pointed, he did so with his whole hand. When he was surprised about something, he turned his palm upside down. When he talked, he held his right thumb in his left palm. When he was angry, he turned away and averted his face. When he was happy, he looked downwards. Generally his laughter consisted of a smile and he showed his teeth which were as white as hailstones.'

Al-Hasan said, 'I refrained from mentioning this to al-Husayn ibn 'Ali for a time. Then I spoke to him and found that he had beaten me to it. He had asked our father about how the Messenger of Allah behaved at home and when he was out, and about his features. He had not omitted anything.

'Al-Husayn said, "I asked my father about how the Messenger of Allah was at home.

"He said, 'It was allowed him to enter his house for his own comfort. When he retired to his house, he divided his time into three parts – one part for Allah, one for his family and one for himself. Then he divided his part between his people and himself. He used the time for the people more for the common people than for the elite. He did not reserve anything for himself to their exclusion. Of his conduct in the part reserved for himself was that he would show preference to the people of merit, and would divide the time according to their excellence in the *deen*. Some people needed one thing, some needed two, and some had many needs. He concerned himself with them and kept them busy doing things that were good for them and the community. He always asked about them and what was happening to them. He used to say, "Those who are present should convey things to those who are absent and you should let me know what is needed by people who cannot convey their needs to me. On the Day of Rising, Allah will make firm the feet of a person who conveys to a ruler the need of someone who cannot convey it himself."'" This was all that was mentioned in his presence and he would only accept this from people.'

The *hadith* of Sufyan ibn Wukay' says, 'They entered as seekers and only parted after having tasted something, leaving as guides,' i.e. as men of *fiqh*.

'Al-Husayn said, "Tell me about when he went out and how he behaved then."

'His father replied, "The Messenger of Allah, may Allah bless him and grant him peace, held his tongue except regarding what concerned people. He brought people together and did not split them. He honoured the nobles of every group of people and appointed them over their people. He was cautious about people and on his guard against them, but he did that without averting his face from them or being discourteous. He asked about his Companions and he asked people how other people were. He praised what was good and encouraged it, and disliked what was ugly and discouraged it. He took a balanced course, without making changes. He was not negligent, fearing that people would become negligent or weary. He was prepared for any eventuality. He did not neglect a right nor did he let his debts reach the point where others had to help him. The best and most preferred people in his eyes were those who had good counsel for all. Those he most esteemed were those who supported and helped him."

'Al-Husayn then asked him about his assembly and how he behaved in it.

'He said, "The Messenger of Allah, may Allah bless him and grant him peace, did not sit down or stand up without mentioning Allah. He did not reserve a special place for himself and forbade other people to do so. When he came to people, he sat down at the edge of the assembly and he told other people to do the same. He gave everyone who sat with him his share so that no one who sat with him thought that anyone was honoured more than he was. If anyone sat with him or stood near him to ask for something, he put up with that person until the person turned away. When someone asked him for something he needed, he either departed with it or with some consoling words. He had the kindest and best behaviour of all people, being like a father to them. They were all equal in respect of their rights with him.

"His assembly was one of forbearance, modesty, patience and trust. Voices were not raised in it nor were shortcomings made public nor lapses exposed. Its members were attached to each other by fear of Allah and were humble. The old were respected and mercy was shown to the young. They helped those with needs and showed mercy to strangers."

'Al-Husayn then asked about how the Messenger of Allah behaved with his companions.

"Ali said, "The Messenger of Allah, may Allah bless him and grant him peace, was always cheerful, easy-tempered, mild. He was neither rough nor coarse. He did not shout nor utter obscenities. He did not find fault with nor over-praise people. He ignored what was superfluous and left it. He abandoned three things in himself: hypocrisy, storing things up, and what did not concern him. He also abandoned three things in respect of other people: he did not censure anyone, he did not scold them, nor try to find out their secrets.

"He only spoke about things for which he expected a reward from Allah. When he spoke, the people sitting with him were as still as if there were birds on their heads. When he was silent, they talked, but did not quarrel in his presence. When someone talked in front of him, they kept quiet until he had finished. Their conversation was about the first topic broached. He laughed at what they laughed at and was surprised at what surprised them. He was patient with a stranger who had coarse language. He said, 'When you find someone asking for something he needs, then give it to him. He did not look for praise except to counterbalance something. He did not interrupt anyone speaking until that person had himself come to an end by either speaking or getting up from where he was sitting.'"

This is the end of the *hadith* of Sufyan ibn Wukay'.

Someone else asked 'Ali what the silence of the Messenger of Allah was like.

He said, 'He was silent for four reasons: forbearance, caution, appraisal, and reflection. His appraisal lay in constantly observing and listening to the people. His reflection was upon what would endure and what would vanish. He had forbearance in his patience. Nothing provocative angered him.

'He was cautious about four things: in adopting something good which would be followed, in abandoning something bad which would be abandoned, in striving to determine what would be beneficial for his community and in establishing for them what would combine the business of this world and the next.' (*Ash-Shifa'* of Qadi 'Iyad: 1.2.25).

During the last twenty-three years of his life – the period during which the Qur'an was revealed – several attempts were made to kill *sayyedina* Muhammad, may Allah bless him and grant him peace, both in Makka and in Madina, and both on and off the battlefield. Most of the attempts on the battlefield were made by the idol worshippers. Most of the attempts off the battlefield were made by the Jews, whose predecessors, as we have already seen in *Volume Two*, had already successfully killed *sayyedina* Zakariyya and *sayyedina* Yahya, peace be on them, and who but for the grace of Allah might well have succeeded in killing *sayyedina* 'Isa as well, peace be on him.

The degree of patience and forgiveness which *sayyedina* Muhammad displayed towards those who wished him dead, may Allah bless him and grant him peace, is in itself proof of his prophethood and an indication of the vastness of the character which he possessed, as these passages from *Ash-Shifa'* of *Qadi* 'Iyad demonstrate:

> Forbearance, long-suffering, pardoning in spite of having the power to punish and patient endurance in affliction are distinct from each other. Forbearance (*hilm*) is a state of dignified bearing and constancy despite provocation. Long-suffering (*ihtimal*) is self-restraint and resignation in the face of pains and injuries. Patience (*sabr*) is similar to it, but its meaning is slightly different. As for pardoning (*'afw*), it is refusing to hold something against someone else.
>
> All of these qualities are part of the *adab* with which Allah endowed His Prophet. Allah says, **'Take the way of pardon and command the correct and turn away from the ignorant.' (7.199).** It is related (in the *tafsir* of Ibn Jarir and Ibn Abi Hatim) that when this was revealed to the Prophet, he asked Jibril to interpret it for him. Jibril told him, 'Wait until I ask the One Who Knows.' He left and then came back to him and said, 'O Muhammad, Allah commands you to unite yourself with those who cut you off, and to give to those who refuse to give to you, and to pardon those who are unjust to you.'
>
> Allah told him, **'Be steadfast in the face of what afflicts you,'** (31.17) and, **'Be steadfast as those of resolution among the Messengers were steadfast, (46.35)** and, **'Let them pardon and overlook, (24.22).** He says, **'The one who is steadfast and forgives, that is part of the resolution of affairs,' (42.43).**
>
> The results of his forbearance and long-suffering are quite evident. Every man with forbearance is known to have occasional lapses. The Prophet, however, was only increased in steadfastness when the injury to him was great, and was only

increased in forbearance when faced with an excess of importunate people.

'A'isha said, 'The Messenger of Allah, may Allah bless him and grant him peace, was not given a choice between two matters but that he chose the easier of the two as long as it was not a wrong action. If it was a wrong action, he was the furthest of people from it. The Messenger of Allah did not take revenge for himself unless the honour (*hurma*) of Allah was violated. Then he would take revenge for the sake of Allah.' (Al-Bukhari and Muslim).

It is related that when the Prophet had his tooth broken and his face cut on the day of the Battle of Uhud, it was practically unbearable for his Companions. They said, 'If only you would invoke a curse against them.' He replied, 'I was not sent to curse, but I was sent as a summoner and as a mercy. O Allah, guide my people for they do not know.'

It is related that 'Umar said to him, 'My mother and father be your ransom, O Messenger of Allah! Nuh invoked a curse against his people when he said, **'My Lord, do not leave even one of the rejecters upon the earth.'** (71.26). Had you invoked a curse like that against us, we would have been destroyed to the last man. Your back has been trodden on, your face has been bloodied and your tooth has been broken, and yet you have refused to utter anything but good. You have said, "O Allah, forgive my people for they do not know."'

Look at the perfection of bounteousness, degree of virtue (*ihsan*), excellent character, generosity and extreme patience and forbearance exemplified by this statement. The Prophet did not restrict himself to silence regarding them, but pardoned them, was compassionate to them, merciful towards them, supplicated and interceded for them. He said, 'Forgive' or 'Guide', then apologised for their ignorance and said, 'They do not know.'

When a man (a hypocrite called Dhu'l-Huwaysira) said to the Prophet, 'Act fairly. This is a division by which the face of Allah is not desired,' (referring to the distribution of the booty after the Battle of Hunayn), the Prophet did not go further than making it clear to him how ignorant he was, admonishing and reminding him of what he had said to him. He said, 'Confound you! Who will be fair if I am not fair? I would fail and be lost if I did not act fairly.' (Al-Bukhari and Muslim). He restrained one of his Companions who wanted to kill him.

Ghawrath ibn al-Harith, whilst he and some other people were talking about the raid of Dhatu'r-Riqa', undertook to assassinate the Messenger of Allah. He found him sitting alone under a tree. The Messenger of Allah did not stop him until he was standing over him with an unsheathed sword in his hand. He said, 'Who will protect you from me?' The Prophet replied, 'Allah.' The sword fell from his hand and the Prophet grabbed it and said, 'Who will protect you from me?' He said, 'Punish in the best manner,' so he left him and pardoned him. He came to his people and said, 'I have come to you from the best of people.' (Al-Bukhari and Muslim).

One of the major reports about his pardoning was his pardoning the Jewess who had poisoned him with the sheep after she had confessed to the poisoning. (Al-Bukhari and Muslim).

He did not punish Labid ibn al-A'zam when he used magic against him although he was informed about it and it was revealed to him with an explanation of what had happened. He did not even chide him, let alone punish him. Nor did he punish 'Abdullah ibn Ubayy and other hypocrites in spite of the seriousness of what they had done and said about him. On the contrary, he said to the person who indicated that one of them should be killed, 'No, let it not be said that Muhammad kills his companions.' (Al-Bukhari and Muslim).

Anas said, 'I was with the Prophet, may Allah bless him and grant him peace, when he was wearing a thick cloak. A bedouin pulled him so violently by his cloak that the edge of the cloak made a mark on the side of his neck. Then he said, 'Muhammad! Let me load up these two camels of mine with the property of Allah that you have in your possession! You will not let me load up from your property or your father's property.' The Prophet was silent and then he said, 'The property is the property of Allah and I am His slave.' Then he said, 'Shall I take retaliation from you, bedouin, for what you have done to me?' He replied, 'No.' The Prophet asked, 'Why not?' The bedouin replied, 'Because you do not pay back a bad action with a bad action.' The Prophet laughed and ordered that one camel be loaded up with barley, and the other camel with dates.' (Al-Bukhari and Muslim).

'A'isha said, 'I never saw the Messenger of Allah, may Allah bless him and grant him peace, ever take revenge for an injustice done to him as long as it was not regarding one of the orders of Allah which must be respected. He never struck anyone with his hand at all except when doing *jihad* in the way of Allah. He never hit a servant or a woman.' (Al-Bukhari and Muslim).

A man was brought to him and he was told, 'This man wanted to kill you.' The Prophet said, 'Have no fear! Have no fear! Even though you wanted to do that, you would not have been given power over me.' (Ibn at-Tabarani and Ahmad ibn Hanbal).

Before he was a Muslim, Zayd ibn Sa'na came to him demanding that he repay a debt to him. He pulled his garment from his shoulder, seized hold of him and behaved coarsely to the Prophet, saying, 'Banu 'Abdu'l-Muttalib, you are procrastinating.' 'Umar chased him off and spoke harshly to him while the Prophet merely smiled. The Messenger of Allah said, "Umar, he and I need something else from you. Command me to repay well and command him to ask for his debt well.' Then he said, 'I still owe him three.' 'Umar commanded that he be paid and he added twenty *sa'* more since he had alarmed him. That, according to Zayd's explanation, was the reason for him becoming Muslim. He said, 'There were only two remaining signs of prophethood which I had not yet recognised in Muhammad or noticed: forbearance overcoming quick-temperedness and extreme ignorance only increasing him in forbearance. I tested him for these and I found him as described.' (Al-Bayhaqi).

The *hadiths* about his forbearance, patience, and pardon in spite of having power to punish are too many to present. Those we have mentioned should be sufficient. They can be found in the *Sahih* collections and other reliable books transmitted by many paths of transmission. They deal with his patience in the face of Quraysh's harshness and the injury done to him in the *Jahiliyyah* and his endurance of great hardships at the hands of Quraysh until Allah let him conquer them and gave him power over them. They did not doubt that they would be wiped out and their wealthy men killed, but he kept on pardoning and overlooking. He said, 'What do you say I have done to you?' They replied, 'Good – a generous brother and a generous nephew.' He said, 'I say as my brother Yusuf said, **'No reproach will be upon you.'** (12.92). Go, you are free.'

Anas said, 'Eight men from Tan'im came to the dawn prayer with the intention of killing the Messenger of Allah, may Allah bless him and grant him peace. They were seized and the Messenger of Allah set them free. Allah revealed, **"He is the One Who restrained their hands from you."** **(48.24)**. (Muslim).

When Abu Sufyan was brought to him – after he had brought the Confederates against him, killed his uncle and Companions, and made a punitive example of them – the Prophet forgave him and was gentle to him. He said, 'Confound you, Abu Sufyan! Isn't it high time that you knew that there is no god but Allah?' He said, 'My father and mother be your ransom! How forbearing and generous you are, maintaining ties of kinship!' (At-Tabarani and al-Bayhaqi).

The Messenger of Allah was the slowest person to anger and the easiest to please, may Allah bless him and grant him peace.' (*Ash-Shifa'* of *Qadi* 'Iyad: 1.2.12).

And:

> An instance of his compassion was that he called on his Lord and made a compact with Him saying, 'If ever I curse a man or make an invocation against him, make it *zakat* for him and mercy, prayer, purification and an act of drawing near by which he will draw near to You on the Day of Rising.' (Al-Bukhari and Muslim).
>
> When his people rejected him, Jibril came to him and said, 'Allah has heard what your people say to you and how they reject you. He has ordered the angels of the mountains to obey whatever you tell them to do.' The angel of the mountains called him, greeted him and said, 'Send me to do what you wish. If you wish, I will crush them between the two mountains of Makka.' The Prophet said, 'Rather, I hope that Allah will bring forth from their loins those who will worship Allah alone and not associate anything with Him.' (Al-Bukhari and Muslim). (*Ash-Shifa'* of *Qadi* 'Iyad: 1.2.17).

And:

> Allah put the Prophets to the test by means of various types of affliction in order to increase their position and elevate their rank. Afflictions were the cause which elicited the states of steadfastness, pleasure, thankfulness, submission, reliance entrusting, supplication and entreaty and confirmed the Prophets' insight into mercy towards people who were tested and compassion for those who were suffering affliction. Their afflic-

tion was a reminder and warning for others so that people would emulate the Prophets in affliction and find solace in the trials which befell them and imitate them in steadfastness. Affliction erased any small mistakes into which they had slipped and their acts of heedlessness so that they would meet Allah purified and cleansed and thereby their wage would be more complete and their reward more abundant.

Mus'ab ibn Sa'd said that his father said that he asked the Messenger of Allah, 'Which people have the greatest affliction?' He answered, 'The Prophets, and then the best of men (*al-amthal*). The best of men are those who are tested in accordance with their adherence to the *deen*. Affliction continues to afflict the worshipper until it leaves him walking on the earth free of error.' (At-Tirmidhi). (*Ash-Shifa'* of *Qadi* 'Iyad: 3.2.9).

This indeed is how the Prophet Muhammad, may Allah bless him and grant him peace, left this world in 10 AH / 632 CE, at the age of 63 – pure and free from any error. He was buried where he had died, in the room of his wife, 'A'isha, right next to the simple mosque which he had helped to build with his own blessed hands.

In the years and centuries that followed, the Prophet's Mosque has been enlarged repeatedly, and now surrounds his tomb. As *Qadi* 'Iyad makes clear, the courtesy which is due from those who come to visit *sayyedina* Muhammad at his graveside, in his Mosque, may Allah bless him and grant him peace in it, should also be pure and free from any error:

> Visiting his grave is part of the *Sunna* and is both excellent and desirable. Ibn 'Umar said that the Prophet said, 'My intercession is assured for all who visit me.' (Ibn Khuzayma, al-Bazzar and at-Tabarani).
>
> Anas ibn Malik said that the Messenger of Allah said, 'Anyone who visits me in Madina for the sake of Allah is near me and I will intercede for him on the Day of Rising.' (Al-Bayhaqi).
>
> He said, 'Whoever visits me after my death, it is as if he visited me while I was alive.'
>
> Malik disliked people saying, 'We visited the grave of the Prophet, may Allah bless him and grant him peace.' People have disagreed about the meaning of this statement. It is said that he disliked it because of the Prophet's saying, 'Allah curses

women who visit graves.' (Ibn Hanbal). People relate that the Prophet then said, 'I forbade you to visit graves, but now you can visit them.' (Muslim).

The Prophet said, 'Anyone who visits my grave …' and used the word 'visit'. It is said that this is because the visitor is considered to be better than the one visited. This has no foundation since not every visitor has this quality and so it is not a universal principle. The *hadith* concerning the People of the Garden talks about their 'visit' to their Lord, so it is not forbidden to use this expression in respect of Allah.

Abu 'Imran al-Fasi said, 'Malik disliked anyone saying, "the *tawaf* of the visit", or, "we visited the grave of the Prophet", because people normally use that for visits between themselves, and he did not like to put the Prophet on the same level as other people. He preferred a specific statement like, "we greeted the Prophet, may Allah bless him and grant him peace."'

Moreover, it is merely recommended for people to visit each other whereas there is a strong obligation to visit the grave of the Prophet. 'Obligation' here means the recommendation and encouragement to do that, not the obligation which is a legal duty.

I think the best interpretation is that Malik forbade and disliked the practice of connecting the word 'grave' with the Prophet. He did not dislike people saying, 'we visited the Prophet, may Allah bless him and grant him peace.' This is because of the Prophet's statement, 'O Allah, do not make my grave an idol to be worshipped after me. Allah was very angry with people who took the graves of their Prophets as mosques.' So he omitted the word 'grave' in order to cut off the means and close the door to this wrong action. Allah knows best.

Ishaq ibn Ibrahim, the *faqih*, said that when someone goes on *hajj*, he should go to Madina with the intention of praying in the mosque of the Messenger of Allah, seeking the blessing of seeing his *Rawda*, his *minbar*, his grave, the place where he sat, the places his hands touched and the places where his feet walked and the post on which he used to lean, where Jibril descended to him with the revelation, and the places connected with the Companions and the *Imams* of the Muslims who lived there. He should have consideration for all these things.

Ibn Abi Fudayk said that he heard someone state, 'We have heard that all who stop at the Prophet's grave should recite the *ayah*, **"Allah and His angels bless the Prophet,"** (33.56) and then say, "May Allah bless you, Muhammad." If someone says this seventy times, an angel will call to him, "May Allah bless you!" and all his needs will be taken care of.'

Yazid ibn Abi Sa'id al-Mahri said that he went to 'Umar ibn 'Abdu'l-'Aziz, and when 'Umar bade him farewell, he said, 'I would like you to do something for me. When you reach Madina and see the grave of the Prophet, may Allah bless him and grant him peace, greet him for me with peace.' Another said, 'He used to send such greetings in his letters from Syria.'

One of the early Muslims said, 'I saw Anas ibn Malik come to the Prophet's grave. He stopped and raised his hands so that I thought he was beginning the prayer. He greeted the Prophet and then left.'

Ibn Wahb said that Malik said that when someone greets the Prophet, and makes supplication, he should stand with his face towards the grave, not towards *qibla*, draw near and greet him but not touch the grave with his hands. In *Al-Mabsut*, Malik says, 'I do not think people should stand at the grave of the Prophet, may Allah bless him and grant him peace, but should greet and then depart.'

Ibn Abi Mulayka said, 'Anyone who wants to stand and face the Prophet should face the lamp which is in the *qibla* end of the grave at the Prophet's head.'

Nafi' said, 'Ibn 'Umar used to make the greeting at the grave. I saw him come to the grave a hundred times or more. He would say, "Peace be upon the Prophet, may Allah bless him and grant him peace. Peace be upon Abu Bakr." Then he would leave.' Ibn 'Umar was also seen to put his hand on the seat of the Prophet at the *minbar* and then place his hand on his face.

Ibn Qusayt and al-'Utbi said, 'When the mosque was empty, the Companions of the Prophet used to touch the knob of the *minbar* which was near the grave with their right hands. Then they faced to the *qibla* and made supplication.'

In the *Muwatta'* we find that Malik, according to the transmission of Yahya ibn al-Laythi, used to stand at the grave of the Prophet and would pray on the Prophet, Abu Bakr and 'Umar. According to Ibn al-Qasim and al-Qa'nabi, he made supplication for Abu Bakr and 'Umar. According to Ibn Wahb, Malik said that the greeter should say, 'Peace be upon you, O Prophet, and the mercy of Allah and His blessings.' In *Al-Mabsut*, he greeted Abu Bakr and 'Umar.

Qadi Abu'l-Walid al-Baji said, 'I think that he should supplicate for the Prophet using the term '*salat*' and use a different word for Abu Bakr and 'Umar as Ibn 'Umar indicated.'

Ibn Habib said, 'When you enter the Prophet's mosque, you should say, "In the Name of Allah and peace be upon the Messenger of Allah. Peace be upon us from our Lord. Allah and His angels bless Muhammad. O Allah, forgive us our wrong actions and open for us the gates of Your mercy and Your Garden and preserve us from the accursed *shaytan*!"

'Then you should go to the *Rawda* which is that part of the mosque between the grave and the *minbar*. Pray two *rak'ats* there in which you praise Allah before standing at the grave. Ask Him for the complete fulfilment of the intention which brought you out to visit him and for help in realising it. If your two *rak'ats* are outside the *Rawda*, that is sufficient although it is better if they are in the *Rawda*. The Prophet said, "The area between my house and the *minbar* is one of the meadows (*rawdas*) of the Garden. My *minbar* is on one of the raised gardens of the Garden."

'Then you stand at the grave with humility and respect, and bless him and give what praise you can. You greet Abu Bakr and 'Umar and make supplication for them and do a lot of prayer in the mosque of the Prophet night and day. Do not forget to go to the mosque of Quba' and the graves of the martyrs.'

Malik said in his letter to Muhammad (one of Malik's companions, possibly Muhammad ibn al-Hasan ash-Shaybani who was also one of the companions of Abu Hanifa), 'The Prophet, may Allah bless him and grant him peace, should be greeted when you enter and leave (i.e. the Prophet's mosque).' Muhammad said, 'When you leave the mosque, finish your time there standing at the grave. It is the same when you want to leave Madina.'

Ibn Wahb relates that Fatima said that the Prophet said, 'When you enter the mosque, bless the Prophet, may Allah bless him and grant him peace, and say, "O Allah, forgive me my wrong actions and open the doors of Your mercy to me." When you leave, bless the Prophet, may Allah bless him and grant him peace, and say, "O Allah, forgive me my wrong actions and open the doors of Your overflowing favour to me."'

Muhammad ibn Sirin said, 'When people entered the mosque, they used to say, "May Allah and His angels bless Muhammad.

Peace be upon you, O Prophet, and the mercy of Allah and His blessings. In the Name of Allah we have entered and in the Name of Allah we have gone out. We have relied on Allah." They said something similar when they went out.'

When the Messenger of Allah entered the mosque, he used to say, 'O Allah, open the doors of Your mercy to me and make the gates of Your provision easy for me.'

Abu Hurayra said, 'When one of you enters the mosque, let him pray on the Prophet and say, "Allah, open the way for me!"'

In *Al-Mabsut*, Malik said, 'It is not necessary for the people of Madina who enter and leave the mosque to stand at the grave. That is for strangers.'

He also said, 'There is no harm in someone who comes from a journey or leaves on a journey standing at the grave of the Prophet, may Allah bless him and grant him peace, and asking for blessing on him and making supplication for him and for Abu Bakr and 'Umar.' He was told that some of the people of Madina who had neither come from a journey nor were going on a journey would do that once a day or more, sometimes once or twice on *jumu'a* or other days, giving the greeting and making supplication for an hour. Malik said, 'I have not heard this mentioned by any of the people of *fiqh* in our city. It is permitted to abandon it. The last people of this community are only put right by the first, and I have not heard of the first people of this community or any of the *Salaf* doing that. It is disliked except for someone who has come from or is going on a journey.'

Ibn al-Qasim said, 'When the people of Madina left or entered Madina, I saw that they used to come to the grave and give the greeting.' He said, 'That is what is considered to be the correct thing to do.'

Al-Baji said, 'There is a difference between the people of Madina and strangers because strangers have a specific intention for doing so whereas the Madinans live there and do not intend to go there for the sake of the grave and the greeting.'

In the book of Ahmad ibn Sa'id al-Hindi about people standing at the grave we find, 'Do not cling to it and do not touch it and do not stand at it for a long time.'

In the *'Utbiyya* we find, 'In the mosque of the Prophet, may Allah bless him and grant him peace, begin with the prayer on the Prophet which you say before the *salam*.

'The best place for *nafila* prayers in the mosque of the Prophet is in the prayer-place of the Prophet where the post scented with *khaluq* perfume is located. In the obligatory prayer, it is best to go to the front rows. I prefer strangers to do the *nafila* prayers there rather than in their houses.' (*Ash-Shifa'* of *Qadi* 'Iyad: 3.2.9).

It is equally important, for your own good in this world and in the next, to have the respect and love which is due to the Prophet Muhammad, may Allah bless him and grant him peace, in your own heart, wherever you may happen to be:

It is just as necessary to have esteem and respect for the Prophet after his death as it was when he was alive. This means to show it whenever the Prophet, his *hadith* or *sunna* are mentioned, when anyone hears his name or anything about his life or how his family and relatives behaved. It includes respect for the People of his House (*ahl al-bayt*) and his Companions.

Abu Ibrahim at-Tujibi said, 'It is obligatory for every believer to be humble, fearful, show respect and be still when they mention the Prophet or the Prophet is mentioned in their presence. They should be as respectful as they would have been if they had actually been in his presence taking on the *adab* which Allah taught us.' That is the way our right-acting *Salaf* and past *Imams* behaved.

Abu Humayd said, 'Abu Ja'far, the *Amir al-Mu'minin*, had a dispute with Malik in the Prophet's mosque. Malik said to him, "*Amir al-Mu'minin*, do not raise your voice in this mosque. Allah taught the people how to behave by saying, **'Do not raise your voices above the Prophet.'** (49.2). He praises people with the words, **'those who lower their voices in the presence of the Messenger of Allah,** (49.3). He censures people, saying, **'those who call out to you,'** (49.4). Respect for him when he is dead is the same as respect for him when he was alive."

'Abu Ja'far was humbled by this. He asked Malik, "Abu 'Abdullah, do you face *qibla* when you supplicate or do you face the Messenger of Allah?" He replied, "Why would you turn your face from him when he is your means and the means of your father, Adam, to Allah on the Day of Rising? I face him and ask him to intercede and Allah will grant his intercession. Allah says, **'If, when they had wronged themselves, they had come to you …'"'** (4.64). (*Ash-Shifa'* of *Qadi* 'Iyad: 2.3.3).

Elsewhere in his *Ash-Shifa'*, Qadi 'Iyad states:

> Ibn 'Abbas said, 'Some of the Companions of the Prophet sat down to wait for him. He came out and stood near them and heard what they were saying to one another. One of them said, "How extraordinary! Allah took Ibrahim from among His creation as His close friend." Another said, "Even more extraordinary was when Allah spoke directly to Musa!" Another said, "'Isa is the word of Allah and His spirit!" Another said, "Allah chose Adam!"
>
> 'Then the Prophet came and greeted them and said, "I have heard what you were saying and noticed your amazement at the fact that Allah chose Ibrahim as a close friend, and it is the case; that Musa is the intimate of Allah, and it is the case; that 'Isa is the spirit of Allah, and it is the case; and that Adam was chosen, and it is the case. I am the beloved of Allah and it is no boast. I will be the first to intercede and the first whose intercession is accepted, and it is no boast. I am the first who will knock at the gate of the Garden and Allah will open it for me and let me enter it along with the poor among the believers, and it is no boast. I am the most honoured of the first and the last, and it is no boast."' (At-Tirmidhi). (*Ash-Shifa'* of *Qadi 'Iyad: 1.3.9*).

And:

> Abu Dharr, Ibn 'Umar, Ibn 'Abbas, Abu Hurayra and Jabir ibn 'Abdullah related that he said, 'I have been given five things which no Prophet before me was given. I have been helped by terror being cast in the hearts of my enemies a month in advance of my arrival. The earth has been made a mosque for me and a place of purity so that when the time of the prayer comes, any man of my community can pray. Spoils of war, which were not made lawful for any Prophet before me, have been made lawful for me. I have been sent to all people. I have been given intercession.'
>
> Another version includes, 'Ask and you will be given it.' In yet another version, 'My community will be presented before me and I will have no fear about what can come to the followed from the follower.'
>
> One version has, 'I was sent to the red and the black.' It is said that the black are the Arabs and the red are the foreigners. It is said that the red are men and the black are the *jinn*.

Another *hadith* from Abu Hurayra says, 'I have been helped by terror being cast into the hearts and I have been given all the words. While I was asleep, I dreamt that the keys of the treasures of the earth were brought and placed in my hands.' One variant has, 'The Prophets were sealed by me.'

'Uqba ibn 'Amir said that the Prophet said, 'I will go ahead on your behalf and I will be a witness for you. By Allah, I am looking at the *Hawd* even now. I have been given the keys to the treasures of the earth. By Allah, I do not fear that you will associate partners (with Allah) after me, but I fear that you will contend with each other for this world.' (Al-Bukhari and Muslim).

'Abdullah ibn 'Amr said that the Messenger of Allah said, 'I am Muhammad, the unlettered Prophet. There is no Prophet after me. I was given all the words and their seals. I was made to recognise the guardians of the Fire and the bearers of the Throne.' (Ahmad ibn Hanbal).

Ibn 'Umar said that the Prophet said, 'I was sent not long before the Last Hour.' (Ahmad ibn Hanbal, and Al-Bukhari and Muslim from Anas).

Ibn Wahb said that the Prophet said, 'Allah said, "Ask, O Muhammad!" I said, "What shall I ask for, my Lord? You took Ibrahim as a friend; You spoke directly to Musa; You chose Nuh; and You gave Sulayman a kingdom which no one after him can have." Allah said, "What I have given you is better than that. I have given you *Kawthar*, and I have placed your name alongside My Name which is called out in the heavens. I have made the earth a place of purity for you and for your community. I have forgiven you your past and future wrong actions. You walk among people who are forgiven because of you. I have not done this for anyone before you. I have made the hearts of your community their Qur'ans. I have stored up your intercession for you and I have not stored it up for any Prophet but you."' (Al-Bayhaqi). (*Ash-Shifa'* of *Qadi* 'Iyad: 1.3.1).

Qadi 'Iyad's summary of the most reliable *hadith* concerning the Last Day and the Prophet Muhammad's intercession on behalf of his community on that Day – may the blessings and peace of Allah be on him and on his family and companions and on all who follow him and them with sincerity – is most illuminating:

Allah says to the Prophet, **'Perhaps your Lord will raise you up to a praiseworthy station.'** **(17.79)**.

Adam ibn 'Ali heard Ibn 'Umar say, 'People will arrive kneeling on the Day of Rising. Every community will follow their Prophet, saying, 'O so-and-so! Intercede for us!' until intercession comes to the Prophet. That is the day when Allah will raise him to the Praiseworthy Station.' (Al-Bukhari).

Abu Hurayra said that the Messenger of Allah was asked about the words of Allah, **'Perhaps your Lord will raise you up to a praiseworthy station.'** **(17.79)**. He said, 'It means intercession.' (Ibn Hanbal and al-Bayhaqi).

Ka'b ibn Malik related that the Prophet said, 'People will be gathered on the Day of Rising, and my community and I will be on a hill and my Lord will clothe me in a green robe and give me permission. Then I will say what Allah wills I say. That is the Praiseworthy Station.' (Ahmad ibn Hanbal).

Ibn 'Umar mentioned the *hadith* about intercession and said, 'He will advance until he knocks at the gates of the Garden. On that day, Allah will grant him the Praiseworthy Station He promised him.'

Ibn Mas'ud said, 'The Prophet will stand on the right of the Throne in a station where none but he will stand. The first and the last will envy it.' (Ibn Hanbal).

Ibn Mas'ud said that the Messenger of Allah said, 'I will stand in the Praiseworthy Station.' He was asked, 'What is it?' He said, 'On that day, Allah will descend on His Throne ...' (*hadith* in Ibn Hanbal).

Abu Musa al-Ash'ari said that the Prophet said, 'I was given a choice between having half of my community enter the Garden, or being granted intercession. I chose intercession because it is more encompassing. Do you think that it is on behalf of those who fear Allah? It is for those who err and commit wrong actions.' (Ibn Majah).

Abu Hurayra said, 'I asked, "Messenger of Allah! What has come to you about intercession?" He replied, "My intercession is for the one who testifies that there is no god but Allah sincerely, his tongue confirming what is in his heart."' (Al-Bayhaqi).

Umm Habiba said that the Messenger of Allah said, 'I was shown what would happen to my community after me and that they would shed each other's blood and that what had happened to previous communities from Allah would also happen to them. Therefore I asked Allah to grant me intercession on their behalf on the Day of Rising, and He did that.' (Al-Hakim and al-Bayhaqi).

Hudhayfa said, 'Allah will gather people together on one vast plain where, after hearing the summoner, they will all appear. They will be barefoot and naked as when they were created. They will be silent and no one will speak except by His permission. There will be a call, "Muhammad!" He will reply, "At your service! Good is in Your hands and evil is not (attributed) to You! The one You guide is guided and Your slave is in Your presence, Yours, to You. There is no place of safety or refuge from You except with You. You are Blessed and Exalted. Glory be to You, the Lord of the House."' Hudhayfa continued, 'That is the Praiseworthy Station which Allah has spoken of.' (Al-Bayhaqi and an-Nasa'i).

Ibn 'Abbas said, 'As the people of the Fire enter the Fire and the people of the Garden enter the Garden, and only the last company of the Garden and the last company of the Fire are left, the company of the Fire will say to the company of the Garden, "Your belief has not helped you." They will call on their Lord, bellowing, and the people of the Garden will hear them, and they will ask Adam and the Prophets after him to intercede on their behalf. Each of the Prophets will make some excuse until they come to Muhammad. He will intercede for them. That is the Praiseworthy Station.'

Jabir ibn 'Abdullah said to Yazid al-Faqir (ibn Suhayb), 'Have you heard about 'the station of Muhammad'?' (i.e. the station which Allah will grant him). He replied that he had and said, 'It is the Praiseworthy Station of Muhammad by means of which Allah will bring out of the Fire whoever comes out of it,' and he mentioned the *hadith* of intercession about bringing the people out of *Jahannam*. (Muslim). Anas said that this refers to the Praiseworthy Station which the Prophet was promised.

In the version of Anas, Abu Hurayra and others, the Prophet said, 'Allah will join the first and the last on the Day of Rising and they will be anxious – or consumed. They will say, "If only we could seek intercession with our Lord!"' (One variant has, 'People will surge against each other.'). (Al-Bukhari and Muslim).

Abu Hurayra said, 'The sun will draw close and people will feel such intense distress that they will not be able to bear it. They will say, "Is there no one to intercede for us?" They will come to Adam and say, "You are Adam, the father of mankind. Allah created you with His hand and breathed some of His spirit into you and let you dwell in His Garden and made the angels prostrate to you and taught you the names of everything. Intercede for us with your Lord so that He will rescue us from the position we are in. Don't you see what we are going through?" He will say, "My Lord is angry today with such an anger that has never been before and which will never be again. He forbade me the Tree and I rebelled. O my soul! My soul! Go to someone else. Go to Nuh."

'They will come to Nuh and say, "You are the first of the Messengers to be sent to the people of the earth and Allah called you a thankful slave. Don't you see what we are going through? Would you intercede for us with your Lord?" He will say, "My Lord is angry today with such an anger that has never been before and will never be again. O my soul! My soul!" (In Anas' version, he mentioned the error which he had committed when he asked his Lord without knowledge. In Abu Hurayra's version, he said, 'I made a supplication on behalf of my family.') "Go to someone else. Go to Ibrahim. He is the close friend of Allah."

'They will come to Ibrahim and say, "You are the Prophet of Allah and His close friend from among the people of the earth. Intercede with your Lord for us! Don't you see what we are going through?" He will say, "My Lord is angry today with such an anger that has never been before and will never be again." (And he mentioned the lies that he told: when he said, 'I am ill,' when summoned to the idols; when he said to the king that his wife was his sister; and when he said that the biggest of the idols had done the deed. However, all these are true when interpreted properly.) "O my soul! My soul! I cannot do it. You must go to Musa. He is the *Kalim* of Allah." (One version has, 'He is a slave to whom Allah gave the Torah and spoke directly and whom He made a near confidant.').

'They will come to Musa and he will say, "I cannot do it," and he will mention the error he committed by killing a person. "O my soul! My soul! You must go to 'Isa. He is the Spirit of Allah and His Word."

'They will come to 'Isa and he will say, "I cannot do it. You must go to Muhammad, a slave whose past and future wrong actions have been forgiven."

'They will come to me and I will say, "I will do it. I will go and ask permission from my Lord and He will give me permission." When I see Him, I will fall down in prostration.' (One version has, 'I will come under the Throne and fall down in prostration,' and in another, 'I will stand before Him and praise Him with praises such as I could not articulate if Allah had not inspired me.' In yet another, 'Allah will open up His praises to me, praises of an excellence not granted to anyone before me.'). (Al-Bukhari and Muslim).

In the version of Abu Hurayra we find, 'It will be said, "Muhammad, lift up your head. Ask and it will be given to you. Intercede and your intercession will be granted." The Prophet said, "I will raise my head and say, 'O Lord, my community! O Lord my community!'" He will say, "Bring in by the right-hand gate those of your community who will not be subjected to reckoning, and the rest of your community can share with people in the other gates."'

This section is not mentioned in Anas' version. Instead he says, 'Then I will fall down in prostration and I will be told, "Muhammad, lift up your head! Speak and you will be heard. Intercede and it will be granted. Ask and you will be given!" I will say, "O Lord, my community! O Lord, my community!" It will be said. "Go and bring out whoever has as much as a barley-grain of belief in his heart." I will go and do that. Then I will return to my Lord and praise Him with those praises. Then Allah will tell me to bring out whoever has the smallest mustard-seed of belief and I will do that.'

Then he mentioned the fourth time and said, 'I will be told, "Lift up your head! Speak and you will be heard. Intercede and it will be granted. Ask and you will be given!" I will say, "O Lord, give me permission for the one who says, 'There is no god but Allah'." He will say, "That is not your affair, but by My might, My pride, My immensity and My greatness, I will bring out of the Fire those who say, 'There is no god but Allah'." (In the version of Qatada, he said, 'I do not know if it was the third or fourth time.'). I will say, "O Lord, let the only ones who remain in it be those whom the Qur'an has barred."' i.e. those obliged to remain in it endlessly. (See, for example, Qur'an 4.14, 4.116 and 4.145.).

Similar *hadiths* are related from Abu Bakr, 'Uqba ibn 'Amr, Abu Sa'id al-Khudri and Hudhayfa. Hudhayfa said, 'They will come to Muhammad and permission will be granted to him. Then trust (*amana*) and kinship will come and stand on both sides of the *Sirat*.'

In the version of Abu Malik from Hudhayfa it says, 'They will come to Muhammad and he will intercede. The *Sirat* will be set up and the first of them will pass over like lightning, the next like the wind, the next like a bird and the next running, while our Prophet, may Allah bless him and grant him peace, is on the *Sirat* saying, "O Allah! Grant safety! Grant safety!" until all the people have gone across.' (Ibn Abi Da'ud).

In Abu Hurayra's version, he said, 'I will be the first to pass over.'

Ibn 'Abbas said that the Prophet said, '*Minbars* will be set up for the Prophets on which they will sit. My *minbar* will remain, but I will not sit on it and will remain standing before my Lord. Allah will ask, "What do you want Me to do with your community?" I will reply, "O Lord, make their reckoning quick." He will call for them and they will be judged. Some of them will enter the Garden by His mercy and some of them will enter the Garden by my intercession. I will continue to intercede until He gives a paper of good deeds to men who have been commanded to the Fire. The Guardians of the Fire will say, "Muhammad! You have not left any scope for the anger of your Lord against your community!"' (Al-Bayhaqi).

From a path of transmission through Ziyad an-Numayri, Anas said that the Messenger of Allah said, 'I am the first from whose skull the earth will part (i.e. on the Day of Rising), and it is no boast. I am the master of the people on the Day of Rising, and it is no boast. The Banner of Praise will be with me on the Day of Rising and I will be the first for whom the Garden will open, and it is no boast. I will knock at the gate of the Garden and it will be said, "Who is this?" and I will say, "Muhammad." It will open for me and the Majestic will receive me and I will fall down in prostration.' (Al-Bayhaqi and Abu Nu'aym).

The version of Unays al-Ashhali has in it, 'I heard the Messenger of Allah say, "I will intercede on the Day of Rising for most of the stones and trees on the earth."' (Ibn 'Abdu'l-Barr).

The general import of these different traditions is that the intercession of the Prophet and his Praiseworthy Station extends from the first intercession to the last. When the people are gathered for the Gathering, and their throats are constricted and they are sweating in the sun, standing all the while before the final Reckoning, he intercedes to allow people relief from the Standing. Then when the *Sirat* is set up and people are judged, he intercedes to hasten to the Garden those among his community who have no reckoning, then he intercedes for those who are to be punished and sent to the Fire, and then he intercedes for those who say, 'There is no god but Allah'. None except the Prophet, may Allah bless him and grant him peace, can do this.

In a sound and famous *hadith* it says, 'Every Prophet has a supplication which he makes. I have reserved my supplication for intercession for my community on the Day of Rising.' (Al-Bukhari and Muslim).

The people of knowledge say that this means that it is a supplication which he knows will be answered for them and that what they desire from it will be obtained. Every Prophet has a supplication which is answered. Our Prophet, may Allah bless him and grant him peace, has one whose worth cannot be reckoned. However, when the Prophets make a supplication, they waver between hope and fear. The answer of a supplication is guaranteed for them in what they wish to ask for so long as they are sure it will be answered.

Muhammad ibn Ziyad and Abu Salih al-Basri related from Abu Hurayra, 'Every Prophet has a supplication which he uses for his community and which is answered. I want to delay my supplication to use as intercession for my community on the Day of Rising.' In Abu Salih's version, 'Every Prophet has a supplication which is answered, but every other Prophet has already used his supplication.'

This supplication is particular to this community and its answer is guaranteed. The Prophet said that he asked for certain things in the *deen* and this world for his community and that some of them were granted and some of them were withheld. He has stored up this supplication for them for the Day of Poverty, the Seal of all Afflictions, the Time of Unanswerable Questions and Unquenchable Desires (i.e. the Last Day of Reckoning). May Allah repay him with the best that a Prophet can be repaid with from his community! May Allah bless him and grant him peace abundantly! (*Ash-Shifa'* of *Qadi* 'Iyad: 1.3.10).

Just as *sayyedina* Muhammad will have the highest station on the Last Day, so he will have the highest station in the Garden, may Allah bless him and grant him peace:

> 'Abdullah ibn 'Amr ibn al-'As said that he heard the Prophet say, 'When you hear the *mu'adhdhan*, then say the same as he says and ask for blessings on me. Whoever blesses me once, Allah will bless him ten times. Then ask Allah to give me the *wasila*, for that is a station in the Garden which is designated for only one of the slaves of Allah and I hope that I will be that one. Whoever asks Allah for this *wasila* will receive intercession.' (Abu Da'ud).
>
> In another *hadith* from Abu Hurayra, 'The *wasila* is the highest degree in the Garden.'
>
> Anas said that the Messenger of Allah said, 'While I was travelling in the Garden, a river appeared before me whose banks were domes of pearls. I asked Jibril, "What is this?" He replied, "This is *Kawthar* which Allah has given you." Then he struck the earth with his hand and brought out musk.' (Al-Bukhari and Muslim).
>
> 'A'isha and 'Abdullah ibn 'Amr relate a similar *hadith* in which he said, 'It flows over pearls and rubies and its water is sweeter than honey and whiter than snow.' One version has, 'When it flows, it does not cut a ravine. There is a basin (the *Hawd*) to which my community will come.'
>
> There is a similar hadith from Ibn 'Abbas, and he also said, '*Kawthar* is the abundant good which Allah gave him.' (Al-Bukhari). Sa'id ibn Jubayr said, 'It is the river which is in the Garden from the good which Allah gave him.'
>
> Hudhayfa said regarding what the Prophet, may Allah bless him and grant him peace, mentioned that he had received from his Lord, 'He has given me *Kawthar*, a river in the Garden which flows into my *Hawd*.'
>
> Ibn 'Abbas said about the words of Allah, **'Your Lord will give to you and you will be satisfied,'** (94.5) that there are a thousand castles of pearl whose earth is musk and which contain what is appropriate for them to contain. A variant version states that they contain the wives and servants which are appropriate for him. (*Ash-Shifa'* of *Qadi* 'Iyad: 1.3.11).

It is now over fourteen centuries ago since *sayyedina* Muhammad died, may Allah bless him and grant him peace in his grave, and although attempts have been made to alter his teachings, both the Qur'an and the record of how he lived still remain intact and alive in the hearts and actions of countless Muslims.

Unlike the teachings of the earlier Prophets, peace be on all of them, which, as we have already seen, have all been changed, some almost beyond recognition, the way of Islam – the way of Muhammad, may Allah bless him and grant him peace – still exists and is still followed, not out of blind faith, but with clear-sighted certainty, a certainty which springs from the knowledge and wisdom which *sayyedina* Muhammad was given and which he transmitted to his family and companions, may the blessings and peace of Allah be on him and them, and which has continued to be transmitted from generation to generation of Muslims ever since that time, right up until the present day.

And one of the foundations of this knowledge and this wisdom is its recognition that all the Prophets were related to each other, peace be on them, that they all brought the same message, that they all followed the same way of life, immersed in the remembrance of and in submission to their Lord, Allah – and that it is only what people have done to their respective teachings at a later stage which often makes them appear so different today:

> **He has commanded you to follow the same *deen* that He decreed for Nuh, and which We have revealed to you (O Muhammad), and which We decreed for Ibrahim, and for Musa, and for 'Isa, saying, 'Establish the *deen* and do not become divided in it.' What you are calling the idol worshippers to follow is dreadful for them, but Allah chooses whomever He wishes for Himself, and He guides whoever turns to Him to Himself. And they did not become divided until after knowledge had come to them, out of rivalry amongst themselves, and if it had not been for a decree for an appointed term which had already come from your Lord, judgement concerning them would certainly have been passed – and surely those who have inherited the Book after them are hopelessly in doubt about it. (42.13-14).**

And this is why the Muslims are commanded as follows:

Say: 'We believe in Allah, and in what has been revealed to us, and in what was revealed to Ibrahim and to Isma'il and to Ishaq and to Ya'qub and to the tribes (of Israel), and in what was given to Musa and 'Isa and the Prophets from their Lord – we make no distinction between any of them, and to Him we have submitted.'

And as for whoever desires a life transaction other than Islam, it will not be accepted from him, and in the next life he will be among the losers. (3.84-85).

And:

O you who believe, as for whoever of you turns away from his *deen*, Allah will replace you with people whom He loves and who love Him, who are humble with the believers and harsh towards the disbelievers, who fight in the way of Allah and who do not fear the blame of anyone who blames – that is the grace of Allah which He grants to whomever He wishes – and Allah is All-Embracing, All-Knowing.

Surely your protection can only be Allah, and His Messenger, and those who believe – those who establish the prayer, and who pay *zakat*, and who bow down in worship – and whoever takes Allah and His Messenger and those who believe as their protection (will know) that surely it is the party of Allah who are victorious. (5.54-56).

And:

Surely those who oppose Allah and His Messenger will certainly be humiliated. Allah has decreed: 'I will certainly be victorious – I and My Messengers – surely Allah is Powerful, Mighty.

You will not find people who believe in Allah and the Last Day loving those who oppose Allah and His Messenger – even if they are their own fathers, or their sons, or their brothers, or their kindred.

As for these, He has decreed that *iman* will be in their hearts, and He has strengthened them with a Spirit from Him, and He will bring them into Gardens underneath which rivers flow, in which they will dwell for ever.

> Allah is pleased with them and they are pleased with Him
> – it is these who are the party of Allah – and is it not the
> party of Allah who are the successful ones? (58.20-22).

Only those who were with the Prophet Muhammad can really know what it was like to be in his blessed company, but the choice which has always faced those who embraced Islam after his death – the choice which faces the Muslims today – is exactly the same as the choice which faced his family and companions on the day that they learned that their beloved Prophet, may Allah bless him and grant him peace, had died:

> And Muhammad is only a Messenger, like the Messengers who went before him, so if he dies or is slain, will you turn back on your heels?
>
> And whoever turns back on his heels will not harm Allah in the least – and Allah will reward those who are grateful.
>
> And no self can die except by the permission of Allah at an appointed time.
>
> And as for whoever wants the reward of this world, We give him some of it, and as for whoever wants the reward of the next world, We give him some of it – and We will reward those who are grateful.
>
> And with how many a Prophet has there been a band of followers who fought with him – and they did not falter in the face of whatever assailed them in the way of Allah, and they did not weaken and they did not give in – and Allah loves those who are steadfast.
>
> And they had nothing to say except to say, 'O our Lord, forgive us our wrong actions and our excesses in our affair, and make our foothold firm, and give us victory over the people who are disbelievers.'
>
> And so Allah gave them the reward of this world and the good reward of the next world – and Allah loves those who are good.
>
> O you who believe, if you obey those who disbelieve, they will make you turn on your heels – and you will turn back as losers – but Allah is indeed your Protector, and He is the Best of Helpers. (3.144-150).

And:

> O you who believe, turn to Allah in sincere repentance – it may be that your Lord will free you from your sins and bring you into Gardens underneath which rivers flow on a Day on which Allah will not disgrace the Prophet and those who believe with him.
>
> Their light will shine ahead of them and on their right and they will say, 'O our Lord, perfect our light for us and forgive us – surely You have power over everything.'
>
> O Prophet, fight the disbelievers and the hypocrites and be harsh with them – their dwelling place will be Jahannam – what an awful journey's end! (66.8-9).

And:

> Surely Allah has bought from the believers their selves and their wealth because the Garden will be theirs. They will fight in the way of Allah, and they will kill and be killed. This is the true promise made by Him in the Taurah and the Ingil and the Qur'an. And who is more true to his promise than Allah? So rejoice in the bargain you have made. And that is the vast success.
>
> Those who turn in repentance, those who worship, those who praise, those who fast, those who bow, those who prostrate, those who enjoin what is right, and who forbid what is wrong, and who keep the limits of Allah – and give good news to the *muminun*. (9.111-112).

And:

> He is the One who has sent His Messenger with guidance and the true *deen* so that it may overcome all other *deens*, however much those who worship idols may detest it.
>
> (9.33).

Allah succinctly summarises the beginning and the middle and the end of the affair – the origin and the nature and the final outcome of the human situation – in Surat az-Zumar:

Allah is the Creator of everything, and He is the Guardian over everything – to Him belong the keys of the heavens and the earth.

And as for those who disbelieve in the signs of Allah – these are the losers.

Say (to them): 'Are you telling me to worship other than Allah? – You fools!'

And it has indeed been inspired in you, as it was in those before you, that, 'If you associate partners (with Allah), then your actions will certainly come to nothing and you will certainly be among the losers.

Indeed, it is Allah you must worship – and be amongst those who are grateful!

And they do not attribute the power to Allah which should rightly be attributed to Him – when the whole earth will be in His hand on the Day of Standing, and the heavens rolled up in His right hand – may He be Glorified and Exalted above what they associate with Him!

And the Trumpet will be blown, and whatever is in the heavens and whatever is in the earth will be struck senseless, with the exception of whomever Allah wishes.

And then it will be blown again – and then they will be standing, waiting, and the earth will shine with the light of her Lord, and the Book will be opened, and the Prophets and the witnesses will be brought forward, and they will be judged by the truth, and they will not be wronged.

And every self will be given exactly what it deserves – and He is best aware of what they do.

And those who disbelieved will be driven towards Hell in crowds, until when they reach it, and its gates are opened, and its keepers say to them, 'Didn't Messengers from among you come to you reciting the signs of your Lord and warning you about your meeting on this Day of yours?' they will reply, 'Yes, indeed,' – but the command of punishment for the disbelievers will still be fulfilled – it will be said (to them), 'Enter the gates of Hell, to dwell there forever!'

> How awful the journey's end is for those who were so proud!
>
> And those who had *taqwa* of their Lord will be led towards the Garden in crowds, until when they reach it, and its gates are opened, its keepers will say to them, 'Peace be on you – you are good, so enter here to live forever.'
>
> And they will say, 'Praise belongs to Allah, the One Who has fulfilled His promise to us and made us inherit this land, dwelling wherever we wish in the Garden.'
>
> How blessed is the reward of those who tried so hard!
>
> And you will see the angels circling around the Throne, hymning the praises of their Lord – and they will be judged by the truth, and it will be said, 'Praise belongs to Allah, the Lord of the worlds!' (39.62-75).

It is in the light of this that the truth of the following *ayah* – which was addressed to *sayyedina* Muhammad, may the blessings and peace of Allah be on him and on his family and on his companions and on all who follow him and them with sincerity in what they are able until the Last Day, as much as everything that has been created in all the worlds – shines through:

> And We did not send you (O Muhammad) except as a mercy to all the worlds. (21.107).

When considering this *ayah*, Qadi 'Iyad states:

> Abu Bakr Muhammad ibn Tahir said in explanation of this *ayah*, 'Allah imbued Muhammad with mercy, so that his very being was mercy and all his qualities and attributes were mercy to all creatures. Whoever is touched by any aspect of his mercy is saved in both worlds from every hateful thing and obtains everything he loves. Do you not see that Allah says, **"We did not send you except as a mercy to all the worlds."** ? (21.107). His life was mercy and his death was mercy. As the Prophet himself said, "My life is a blessing for you and my death is a blessing for you." (Al-Bazzar). The Prophet also said, "When Allah desires mercy for a community, He takes its Prophet to Him before them and He makes him one who goes ahead to prepare the way for them."' (Muslim).

As-Samarqandi explains that the words **'a mercy to all the worlds'** mean for both the *jinn* and mankind. It is also said that it means for all creation. He is a mercy to the believers by guiding them, a mercy to the hypocrites by granting them security from being killed, and a mercy to the unbelievers by deferring their punishment. Ibn 'Abbas said, 'He is a mercy to the believers and also to the unbelievers since they are saved from what befell the other communities who cried lies.' (*Ash-Shifa'* of *Qadi 'Iyad*: 1.1.1).

The Messenger of Allah, *sayyedina* Muhammad, said, 'I have left two matters with you. As long as you hold to them, you will not go the wrong way. They are the *Book of Allah* and the *Sunna* of His Prophet.' (*Al-Muwatta'* of *Imam* Malik: 46.1.3).

The beginning of understanding the knowledge and the wisdom which *sayyedina* Muhammad transmitted – may the blessings and peace of Allah be on him and on his family and on his companions and on all who follow him and them with sincerity in what they are able until the Last Day – is to be found at the beginning of the Qur'an, the Opening Surah:

Surat al-Fatiha

In the Name of Allah the Merciful the Compassionate

**Praise belongs to Allah, Lord of the Worlds,
the Merciful the Compassionate,
King of the Day of the Life-Transaction.
Only You we worship and only You we ask for help.
Lead us on the Straight Path,
The path of those whom You have blessed,
Not of those with whom You are angry,
and not of those who are astray.**

(1.1-7)

Amin

*Allahumma salli ala sayyedina Muhammidan
abdika wa rasulika'n-nabiyyi'l-ummiyy
wa ala alihi wa sahbihi wa sallim*

O Allah, bless our master Muhammad,
Your slave and Your Messenger, the unlettered Prophet,
and his family and his companions and grant them peace.

The Qualities of Muhammad

Muhammad is the fountain-head of lights
and darknesses and the source of their emergence
from the presence of pre-endless-time.

So his light was the first of lights when He determined
the manifestation of His names in the first world.

From him all things were clothed in their origination in
existence, and their continuity is uninterruptedly from him.

The prophets and messengers have come from him
one by one, and all the kings and all the creatures.

The relationship of the Seal and the Poles to his light
is that of a drop to oceans of light and refreshment.

The sun and the moon and the stars have appeared
from him, as have the throne, the tablet of forms,
the footstool and the dynasties.

So witness the light which has spread through existence
and do not see other-than-it, and you will soon arrive.

For he is the highest manifestation of Allah's names
and the perfect secret of the attributes.

So Allah chose him in His timeless knowledge
and sent him to the whole of creation
and to the other messengers.

After awakening him Allah conveyed him one night to
the distance of two bow-spans until he achieved his desire.

The higher world rejoiced when he ascended,
and the throne gave him security from fear.

He perceived the veils and the lights
until he drew near and it was proclaimed:
'Draw near My Beloved, and set aside your shyness.'

'Rejoice in the sight of Our lights
and demand all you want
and it will be given without delay.'

So the Chosen One returned with every noble quality and
he informed the people about al-Aqsa and the paths to it.

Take refuge with him in every dilemma, oh my brother,
and your speech among the people will become like honey.

Delight in hearing of his good character and qualities,
and evoke his virtues, and be on guard against mistakes.

How many miracles have come from his hand? They have
left the envious and all other spiritual teachings powerless.

The greatest of the miracles which were manifested
for him is that Book which brought us deeds.

In every act there are benefits which come from it,
whose number cannot be numbered,
and which are not perceptible to the eyes.

The Book of Allah itself contains some of these benefits
by which every one who is sick of heart
is healed of his sickness.

No hero is capable of his mighty power,
so the inability to praise him is the best of ways.

I have copied you in my praise and I have come
to your compassion seeking intercession with Allah,
so intercede on my behalf.

With Allah you are the greatest of creation in degree, so
bring our hearts closer to what we hope for, oh my desire!

By your rank, created beings serve whoever
seeks shelter with you, oh helper of every *wali*.

O my support! I have sought shelter with you
so do not leave me to my body and my self,
but heal us of our ill feelings.

Nothing befalls the slave whose helper you are:
on the level land and on the mountains you are my staff.

I have become confused about myself,
so take me by the hand.
For me there is no turning away from your first light.

May the God of the throne bless you as long as
the sun of reality is manifested with the names and the acts.

And so with your family and Companions as long as
the grass grows and the sky pours down abundant rain.

Then I ask for acceptance for all the Men of Allah
as long as created beings give praise to the One
Who is above identification with forms.

And unfold all blessings on our brothers, in this world
and the next, and do not abandon us to our actions.

Forgive our parents all their mistakes, and the Muslims,
by an outpouring from You – oh One before-endless-time!

(From the Diwan of Shaykh Muhammad ibn al-Habib)

*Allahumma salli ala sayyedina Muhammidan
abdika wa rasulika'n-nabiyyi'l-ummiyy
wa ala alihi wa sahbihi wa sallim*

O Allah, bless our master Muhammad,
Your slave and Your Messenger, the unlettered Prophet,
and his family and his companions and grant them peace.

❂   ❂   ❂   ❂   ❂

Du'a

*La ilaha il'Allah
sayyiduna Muhammadun rasulu'llah*

*There is no god except Allah
Our master Muhammad is the Messenger of Allah.*

May Allah bless him and his family and grant them peace. O Lord, make us firm by its recital, oh Mawlana, give us results from its invocation. Let us enter into the fortress of its protection – let us be among its people – and let us say it and know it at the time of death. Gather us into the company of our lord and master Muhammad, may Allah bless him and his family and grant them peace, and his Companions and all the believing slaves of Allah.

Amin. Amin. Amin.

And peace be upon the Prophets and the Messengers – and on all the righteous ones.

And peace be upon the Prophets and the Messengers – and on all the righteous ones.

And peace be upon the Prophets and the Messengers – and on all the righteous ones.

And the last of our prayer is: Praise be to Allah, the Lord of the worlds. There is no great power and no strength but through Allah, the Mighty, the Great. My help is only with Allah. In Him I have put my trust – and to Him I turn in renewal. Praise belongs to Allah for the blessing of Islam, and it is blessing enough.

(From the Wird of Shaykh Muhammad ibn al-Habib)

Glossary of Arabic Terms

Allah ta'Ala : Allah the Most High, the Lord of all the worlds. Allah, the supreme and mighty Name, indicates the One, the Existent, the Creator, the Worshipped, the Lord of the Universe. Allah is the First without beginning and the Last without end and the Outwardly Manifest and the Inwardly Hidden.

adab : correct behaviour inward and outward, inner courtesy coming out as graciousness in right action.

adhan : the call to prayer.

ahl al-bayt : 'the people of the House', meaning the Prophet Muhammad's immediate family: Fatima – his daughter, her husband 'Ali – his cousin and son-in-law, and their two sons Hasan and Husayn – his grandsons, may the blessings and peace of Allah be on him and his family – and all their descendants.

ahlu'l-dhimma : non-Muslims living in Muslim territory and under the protection of Muslim rule by virtue of the fact that they have agreed to pay the *jizya* tax.

ahlu'l-kitab : the People of the Book, a term used to refer principally to the Jews and the Christians whose religions are partly based on the Books revealed to *sayyedina* Musa and *sayyedina* 'Isa, peace be on them; a term also used, by extension, to refer to any other group of people who claim to be following a Book revealed by Allah prior to the revelation of the Qur'an.

akhira : the next world, what is on the other side of death, the world after this world in the realm of the Unseen; it is not the life in the *barzakh*, but the life either in the *jannah* or in the *nar*.

'alim : a man of knowledge from amongst the Muslims who acts on what he knows.

amir : one who commands, the source of authority in any given situation.

Amir al-Mu'minin: the 'Commander of the Believers', a title of respect given to the *khalif* of the Muslims.

Ansar: the 'Helpers', the people of Madina who welcomed and aided the Prophet Muhammad and the *Muhajirun*, may the blessings and peace of Allah be on him and them, when he and then they made *hijra* to Madina.

arwah: the plural of *ruh*.

'asr: the obligatory mid-afternoon prayer which can be prayed at any time between mid-afternoon and a little before sunset.

ayah: a sign, a verse of the Qur'an.

ayat: the plural of *ayah*.

baraka: a blessing, any good which is bestowed by Allah, and especially that which increases; a subtle beneficent spiritual energy which can flow through things and people or places. It is experienced in certain places more strongly than in others, and in some places and objects overpoweringly so. Its highest realm of activity is the human being. Purity permits its flow, for it is purity itself, which is Light. Density of perception blocks it. It is transformative, healing and immeasurable.

barzakh: an interspace between two realities which both separates and yet links them; commonly used to describe the interspace between the *dunya* and the *akhira*, which begins when death takes place, when the *ruh* leaves the body – and ends when the Last Day arrives, when the *ruh* and the body are reunited again; also used to describe the realm of the *arwah* in the Unseen, which is the abode of the *ruh* prior to its entering the unborn foetus in the womb after about sixteen weeks of pregnancy.

buraq: the mount on which the Prophet Muhammad made his Night Journey, may Allah bless him and grant him peace.

Dajjal: the false Messiah whose appearance marks the imminent end of the world, the antithesis of Jesus. The science of recognising Dajjal is very intricate and carefully delineated. The manifestation will appear both as a person, and as a certain historical situation, and as a series of cosmic phenomena. Dajjal will affect the masses and cause chaos.

deen : the life-transaction, submission and obedience to a particular system of rules and practices, a debt of exchange between two parties, in this usage between the Creator and the created. Allah says in the Qur'an: **Surely the *deen* with Allah is Islam.** (3.19).

dhikru'llah : remembrance of Allah, invocation of Allah. In a general sense all *'ibada* is dhikru'llah. In common usage it has come to mean invocation of Allah by repetition of His Names or particular formulae. The five pillars of Islam are its foundation. Recitation of the Qur'an is its heart, and invocation of the Single Name, Allah, is its end.

dhimma : obligation or contract, in particular a treaty of protection for non-Muslims living in Muslim territory.

dhuhr : the obligatory mid-day prayer which can be prayed at any time between noon and mid-afternoon.

dinar : a gold coin weighing approximately 4.4 grams.

dirham : a silver coin weighing approximately 3.08 grams.

du'a : making supplication to Allah, asking Allah for whatever you desire.

dunya : the world, not as a cosmic phenomenon but as it is experienced. It derives from a root describing those grapes which appear on the vine but which when you stretch out to pick them prove to be out of reach. Dunya takes on its actuality through attachment. When the heart is liberated, dunya disappears and *akhira*, the next invisible world – appears. Dunya is vanishing and moving away, while the next world is appearing and approaching.

fajr : dawn, first light.

faqih : an *'alim* with a sound knowledge of the *shari'a*, who by virtue of his knowledge is able to make a legal judgement.

Fatiha : the 'Opening', the opening *surah* of the Qur'an.

fitra : the first nature, the natural, primal condition of mankind in harmony with nature.

fuqaha : the plural of *faqih*.

ghusl : ritual washing of the whole body with water alone in order to be pure for the prayer.

hadith : reported speech, particularly of, or about, the Prophet Muhammad, may Allah bless him and grant him peace.

hadith qudsi : those words of Allah on the tongue of His Prophet, may Allah bless him and grant him peace, which are not part of the Revelation of the Qur'an.

hajj : the annual pilgrimage to Makka which every Muslim who has the means and ability must make once in his or her life-time; the performance of the rites of the hajj in the protected area which surrounds the Ka'ba. The hajj is one of the indispensable pillars of Islam.

halal : permitted by the *shari'a*.

hanif : naturally pure, and so only able to worship only Allah.

haqiqa : the truth, reality, Allah.

haram : forbidden by the *shari'a*; also a protected area, an inviolable place, in which certain behaviour is forbidden or necessary.

Haramayn : the two protected areas of *Makka* and *Madina*.

hasan : good.

Hawd : the watering-place of the Prophet Muhammad, may Allah bless him and grant him peace, whose drink will refresh those who have crossed the *Sirat* into the Garden on the Last Day.

Hijr : the semi-circular unroofed enclosure at one side of the Ka'ba, whose low wall outlines the shape of the original Ka'ba built by the Prophet Ibrahim, peace be on him.

hijra : emigration in the way of Allah. Islam takes its dating from the hijra of the Prophet Muhammad, may Allah bless him and grant him peace, from Makka to Madina, in 622 CE.

'ibada : any act of worship.

'Id : a festival; there are two main 'Ids in the Muslim year – the 'Id al-Adha which seals the rites of the *hajj*, and the 'Id al-Fitr which marks the end of the fast of *Ramadan*.

ihram : the conditions of clothing and behaviour adopted by someone on *hajj* or *umrah*.

ihsan : the state of being *hasan*; being absolutely sincere to Allah in oneself; it is to worship Allah as though you see Him, knowing that although you do not see Him, He sees you.

Imam : the one who leads the prayer, a leader who is chosen.

iman : acceptance, belief, trust, in Allah, a gift from Him. Iman is to believe in Allah, His angels, His revealed Books, His messengers, the Last Day, the Garden and the Fire, and that everything is by the Decree of Allah, both the good of it and the bad of it.

'isha : the obligatory night prayer which can be prayed at any time between nightfall and a little before dawn.

Islam : peace and submission to the will of Allah, the way of life embodied by all the Prophets, given its final form in the prophetic guidance brought by the Prophet Muhammad, may Allah bless him and grant him peace. The five pillars of Islam are the affirmation of the *shahada*, doing the *salat*, paying the *zakat*, fasting the month of *Ramadan*, and doing the *hajj* once in a life-time if you are able.

isnad : the record, either memorised or recorded in writing, of the names of the people who form the chain of human transmission, person to person, by means of which a *hadith* is preserved – and accordingly these people themselves. One of the sciences of the Muslims which was developed after the Prophet Muhammad's death, may Allah bless him and grant him peace, is the science of assessing the authenticity of a *hadith* by assessing the reliability of its isnad.

'isra' : the Night Journey of the Prophet Muhammad, may the blessings and peace of Allah be on him, from Makka to Jerusalem and then through the realms of the seven heavens beyond the limit of forms, the *sidrat al-muntaha*, to within two bows' lengths or nearer to the Presence of the Real.

Jabarut : the world of Divine Power.

Jahannam : one of the names of Hell.

jahiliyyah : the time of ignorance, before the coming of Islam.

jamra : a small walled place, but in this usage a stone-built pillar. There are three *jimar* at Mina. One of the rites of the *hajj* is to stone them – as if they were *shaytan*.

Jannah : the Garden, Paradise, the final destination and resting place of the *muminun* in the *akhira*.

Jibril : the angel Gabriel, peace be on him.

jimar : the plural of *jamra*.

jinn : unseen beings created from smokeless fire who co-habit the earth together with mankind.

jizya : the annual tax paid by all healthy adult males of the *ahlu'l-dhimma* who are guaranteed the protection of the Muslims in return.

jumu'a : the day of gathering, Friday, and particularly the jumu'a prayer which is prayed instead of *dhuhr* by all those who are present at the mosque to do the prayer.

Ka'ba : the cube-shaped building at the centre of the Haram in Makka, originally built by the Prophet Ibrahim, peace be on him, and rebuilt with the help of the Prophet Muhammad, may Allah bless him and grant him peace; also known as the House of Allah. The Ka'ba is the focal point which all Muslims face when doing the *salat*. This does not mean that Allah lives inside the Ka'ba, nor does it mean that the Muslims worship the Ka'ba. It is Allah Who is worshipped and Allah is not contained or confined in any form or place or time or concept.

kafir : a person who commits *kufr*, an unbeliever, one who covers up the true nature of existence, the opposite of a *mumin*.

kafirun : the plural of *kafir*.

Kalim : the one to whom Allah spoke directly, meaning the Prophet Musa, peace be on him.

Kawthar: it is said that Kawthar is a river in the Garden, abundant blessing, intercession, and the *Hawd* of the Prophet Muhammad, may Allah bless him and grant him peace.

khalif: someone who stands in for someone else; in this usage, the leader of the Muslim community who stands in as the representative of Allah.

khaluq: a kind of yellowy perfume.

khutba: a speech, and in particular a standing speech given by the *Imam* before the *jumu'a* prayer, and after the two *'Id* prayers.

kufar: the *kafirun*.

kufr: to cover up the truth, to reject Allah and His Messengers, may the blessings and peace of Allah be on him.

kunya: a respectful but intimate way of addressing people as 'the father of so-and-so' or 'the mother of so-and-so'.

la ilaha illa'llah: there is no god but Allah.

Madina: the city, the place of the *deen*, often called Madina al-Munawarra – the illuminated, or the enlightened, city – where the revelation of the Qur'an was completed and in which the Prophet Muhammad died and is buried, may Allah bless him and grant him peace. The first Muslim community was established in Madina al-Munawarra, and Allah says in the Qur'an that this is the best community ever raised up from amongst mankind. Their hearts and intentions and actions were illuminated and enlightened and purified, may Allah be pleased with all of them, through Allah and His Messenger, and today Madina is still illuminated by the presence of the *arwah* of those of them who are buried there – especially the Messenger of Allah, may the blessings and peace of Allah be on him and them – and by the presence of those who follow in their footsteps.

maghrib: the obligatory sunset prayer which should be prayed straight after sunset.

Makka: the city in which the Ka'ba stands, and in which the Prophet Muhammad was born, may Allah bless him and grant him peace, and where the revelation of the Qur'an commenced.

Malakut : the world of forms, intangible and invisible, in the Unseen.

mala'ika : the angels, who are made of light and glorify Allah unceasingly. They are neither male nor female. They do not need food or drink. They are incapable of wrong action and disobedience to Allah. They do whatever Allah commands them to do. Everyone has two recording angels with them who record their actions and none of this escapes the knowledge of Allah.

maqam al-Ibrahim : the station of Ibrahim, the place where the Prophet Ibrahim stood in prayer in front of the Ka'ba, peace be on him, and which marks the place of prayer following *tawaf* of the Ka'ba.

Masjid al-Aqsa : the 'Furthest Mosque' in Jerusalem, built in the 7th century CE, which stands where the Temple of Solomon once stood. The *qibla* of the first Muslim community in Madina was initially towards Jerusalem, until it was replaced by the *qibla* towards Makka, in 2 AH.

Masjid al-Haram : the 'Protected Mosque', the name of the mosque built around the Ka'ba in the Haram at Makka.

Masjid an-Nabiyyi : the 'Prophet's Mosque', the name of the mosque in which is the Prophet Muhammad's tomb, may Allah bless him and grant him peace, in Madina.

mathani : 'often repeated', the seven mathani are usually taken to mean the seven *ayat* of Surat al-Fatiha, the opening *surah* of the Qur'an, which is repeated at least seventeen times a day by every Muslim who does the five obligatory daily prayers.

Mawlana : our Lord.

minbar : steps on which the *Imam* stands to deliver the *khutba* on the day of the *jumu'a*.

mi'raj : the Night Journey of the Prophet Muhammad, may the blessings and peace of Allah be on him, from Makka to Jerusalem and then through the realms of the seven heavens beyond the limit of forms, the *sidrat al-muntaha*, to within two bows' lengths or nearer to the Presence of the Real.

mu'adhdhan : the one who calls the *adhan*.

mudd : a measure of volume, one both hands cupped together full.

Muhajirun : the 'Emigrants', the early companions of the Prophet Muhammad who embraced Islam outside Madina, particularly in Makka, and then made *hijra* to Madina to join him and the *Ansar*, may the blessings and peace of Allah be on him and them.

Muhammad ar-Rasulu'llah : Muhammad is the Messenger of Allah, may the blessings and peace of Allah be on him.

muhsin : someone who possesses the quality of *ihsan*, who remembers Allah constantly.

Mulk : the world of forms, physical and visible, in the Seen.

mumin : a believer, someone who possesses the quality of *iman*, who trusts in Allah and accepts His Messenger, may Allah bless him and grant him peace, and for whom the *akhira* is more real than the *dunya*. The mumin longs for the Garden so much, that this world seems like the Fire by comparison.

muminun : the plural of *mumin*.

munafiq : a hypocrite; the hypocrites amongst the Muslims outwardly profess Islam on the tongue, but inwardly reject Allah and His Messenger, may Allah bless him and grant him peace, siding with the *kafirun* against the Muslims. The deepest part of the Fire is reserved for the *munafiqun*.

munafiqun : the plural of *munafiq*.

mushrik : one who commits *shirk*.

mushrikin : the plural of *mushrik*.

Muslim : whoever follows the way of Islam, doing what is obligatory, avoiding what is forbidden, keeping within the limits prescribed by Allah, following the *sunnah* of the Prophet Muhammad, may Allah bless him and grant him peace, in what he or she is able. A Muslim is, by definition, one who is safe and sound, at peace in this world and promised the Garden in the next world.

nabi: a Prophet, a rightly-guided man sent by Allah to guide others how to live and how to only worship Allah.

nafila: a voluntary act of *'ibada*.

Nar: the Fire of Jahannam, Hell, the final destination and place of torment of the *kafirun* and the *munafiqun* in the *akhira*.

nifaq: hypocrisy.

qadar: the decree of Allah, which determines every sub-atomic particle in existence, and accordingly whatever appears to be in existence. One of Allah's Names is 'al-Qadir' – 'the Powerful, the One Who does what He wants, the One Who has Power over everything'. The Prophet Muhammad, may Allah bless him and grant him peace, said, 'Everything is by decree.' (*Al-Muwatta'* of *Imam Malik*: 46.1.5).

qibla: the direction faced in prayer, which, for the Muslims, is towards the Ka'ba in Makka. Everyone has a direction in life, but only the Muslims have this *qibla*.

qintar: a relatively large measure of weight, about 45 kgs.

qirat: a measure of weight with contrary meanings, either a very small weight of approximately 0.25 gms, or a very great weight like that of a mountain.

Qur'an: the 'Recitation', the last Revelation from Allah to mankind and the *jinn* before the end of the world, revealed to the Prophet Muhammad, may Allah bless him and grant him peace, through the angel Jibril, over a period of twenty-three years, the first thirteen of which were spent in Makka and the last ten of which were spent in Madina. The Qur'an amends, encompasses, expands, surpasses and abrogates all the earlier revelations revealed to the earlier Messengers, peace be on all of them. The Qur'an is the greatest miracle given to the Prophet Muhammad by Allah, for he was illiterate and could neither read nor write. The Qur'an is the uncreated word of Allah. The Qur'an still exists today exactly as it was originally revealed, without any alteration or change or addition or deletion. Whoever recites the Qur'an with courtesy and sincerity receives knowledge and wisdom, for it is the well of wisdom in this age.

rak'a : a unit of the prayer, a complete series of standing, bowing, prostrations and sittings.

rak'at : the plural of *rak'a*.

Ramadan : the month of fasting, the ninth month in the Muslim lunar calendar, during which all adult Muslims who are in good health fast from the first light of dawn until sunset each day. The Qur'an was first revealed in the month of Ramadan. The fast of Ramadan is one of the indispensable pillars of Islam.

rasul : a Messenger, often a *nabi* who was given a revealed Book by Allah.

Rawda : the part of the Prophet's Mosque between his grave and the *minbar*. He said, may Allah bless him and grant him peace, 'What is between my house and my *minbar* is one of the meadows of the Garden, and my *minbar* is on my *Hawd*.' (*Al-Muwatta'* of *Imam* Malik: 14.5.10).

ruh : the spirit which gives life, formed from pure light; also the angel Jibril.

Safa and Marwa : Two small hills situated near the Ka'ba in Makka.

sa'a : a measure of volume equal to four *mudds*.

sahih : healthy and sound with no defects; often used to describe a fully authenticated *hadith*. Two of the most reliable collections of *hadith*, those of Al-Bukhari and Muslim, are both called 'the Sahih'.

sajda : the act of making prostration, particularly in the prayer (*salat* – see below).

Salaf : the 'early years', a term used generally to describe the early generations of the Muslims, particularly the *sahaba*, the companions of the Messenger of Allah, may the blessings and peace of Allah be on him and them.

salat : the prayer, particularly the five daily obligatory ritual prayers of the Muslims which are called *maghrib*, *'isha*, *fajr*, *dhuhr* and *'asr*. They consist of fixed numbers of *rak'at* in worship to Allah. Salat is one of the indispensable pillars of Islam.

sawm: fasting, particularly the fast of Ramadan, from food and drink – and making love if you are married – during daylight, from the first light of dawn until sunset.

sa'y: one of the rites of the *umrah* and of the *hajj*. Sa'y is proceeding between the two hills of *Safa* and *Marwa* seven times, increasing your pace each time you come to a certain point, but not breaking into a run, and then slowing down again.

sayyedina: 'our master', a term of respect.

shahada: to witness, to bear witness that: There is no god but Allah and that Muhammad is the Messenger of Allah, may Allah bless him and grant him peace. The shahada is the gateway to Islam in this world and the gateway to the Garden in the next world. It is easy to say, but to act on it is a vast undertaking which has far-reaching consequences, both in inward awareness and in outward action, both in this world and in the next world. Continual affirmation of the shahada is one of the indispensable pillars of Islam.

shari'a: a road, the legal and social modality of a people based on the revelation of their Prophet. The last shari'a in history is that of Islam. It abrogates all previous shari'as. It is, being the last, therefore the easiest to follow, for it is applicable to the whole human race wherever they are.

shaykh: an old man – an *'alim* who has knowledge of Allah and His Messenger, may Allah bless him and grant him peace, and His *deen* – the one who guides you from knowledge of your self to knowledge of your Lord.

shaytan: a devil, particularly Iblis (Satan), an evil *jinn* who prompts mankind and the *jinn* to rebel against Allah. Shaytan is part of the creation of Allah, and we seek refuge in Allah from the evil that He has created.

shayatin: the plural of *shaytan*.

shirk: the unforgivable wrong action of worshipping something or someone other than Allah or associating something or someone as a partner with Him; the opposite of *Tawhid* which is affirmation of Divine Unity. Shirk is idol-worship, which is attributing form to Allah by attempting to confine Him within an object, a concept, a ritual or a myth – whereas Allah is not like anything and has no form. He cannot be conceived of or perceived.

sidrat al-muntaha : 'the lote-tree of the furthest limit', the place where form ends.

Sirat : the narrow bridge which must be crossed on the Last Day in order to enter the Garden.

Sirat al-Mustaqim : the Straight Path, of Islam, which leads through this world to the Garden in the next world.

subh : the obligatory dawn prayer which can be prayed at any time between *fajr* and a short while before the sun rises.

sunnah : a form, the customary practice of a person or group of people. It has come to refer almost exclusively to the practice of the Messenger of Allah, Muhammad, may Allah bless him and grant him peace, but also comprises the customs of the first generation of Muslims in Madina, who acted in accordance with what they had learned from him and who transmitted what they had learned to the next generation. The sunnah is a complete behavioural science that has been systematically kept outside the learning framework of this society, but which nevertheless has been preserved by those to whom it has been transmitted and who continue to embody it as their way of life. The Messenger of Allah, may Allah bless him and grant him peace, said: "I have left two matters with you. As long as you hold to them, you will not go the wrong way. They are the Book of Allah and the Sunnah of His Prophet." (*Al-Muwatta'* of *Imam Malik*: 46.1.3).

surah : a form, a chapter of the Qur'an, composed of *ayat* linked by thematic content.

tafsir : commentary on the Qur'an.

taqwa : being careful, knowing your place in the cosmos. Its proof is the experience of awe of Allah, which inspires a person to be on guard against wrong action and eager for actions which are pleasing to Him.

tawaf : circling the Ka'ba; tawaf is done in sets of seven circuits followed by two *rak'at* of prayer, preferably at the *maqam al-Ibrahim*.

tawba : returning to correct action after error, turning away from wrong action to Allah and asking His Forgiveness, turning to face the Real whereas before one turned one's back. Your turning to Him is in reality His turning to you.

Tawhid : the Divine Unity, Unity in its most profound sense. Allah is One in His Essence and His Attributes and His Acts. The whole of the creation and what it contains is one unified event which in itself has no lasting reality. Allah is the Real: **Surely we come from Allah and surely to Him we return.** (Qur'an: 2.156).

'ulama' : the plural of *'alim*.

Ummah : a nation, the body of Muslims as one distinct community.

Umm al-Mu'minin : 'Mother of the Believers', an honorary title given to the wives of the Prophet Muhammad, may the blessings and peace of Allah be on him and his family and his companions.

'umrah : the lesser pilgrimage to the Ka'ba in Makka and the performance of its rites in the protected area which surrounds the Ka'ba. You can go on 'umrah at any time of the year.

wahi : revelation; the inspiration placed in the hearts and the minds of the Prophets, may the blessings and peace of Allah be on all of them, by Allah ta'Ala.

wali : a friend of *Allah*, one who has both inward knowledge and outward knowledge – knowledge of the *haqiqa* and of the *shari'a*.

wasila : something which makes something else happen, for example, love; see also, for example Qur'an 5.35; also the highest station with Allah in the Garden, said to be nearest the Throne, which will belong to the Prophet Muhammad, may Allah bless him and grant him peace.

wudu : ritual washing of the hands, mouth, nostrils, face, forearms, head, ears and feet with water alone so as to be pure for the prayer. It is necessary to be in *ghusl* for wudu to be effective.

Yawm al-Qiyama : the Day of Standing, the Last Day, when everyone who has ever lived will be given life again, their actions and intentions in this world weighed in the balance, and their final abode determined; also known as 'Yawm al-Ba'ath' – the Day of Rising, 'Yawm al-Hashr' – the Day of Gathering, 'Yawm al-Qiyama' – the Day of Standing, 'Yawm al-Mizan' – the Day of the Balance, 'Yawm al-Hisab' – the Day of Reckoning, 'Yawm ad-Deen' – the Day of the Life-Transaction, and 'Yawm al-Akhira' – the Day of the Next World. The Last Day will be followed by life in the Garden or the Fire, for ever.

zakat : the wealth tax obligatory on Muslims each year, usually payable in the form of one fortieth of surplus wealth which is more than a certain fixed minimum amount, which is called the *nisab*. Zakat is payable on accumulated wealth, especially gold and silver, merchandise, certain crops, certain livestock, and on subterranean and mineral wealth. As soon as zakat is collected it is redistributed to those in need, as defined in the Qur'an and the *hadith*. Zakat is one of the indispensable pillars of Islam.

zakat al-fitr : a small obligatory head-tax imposed on every responsible Muslim who has the means for himself and his dependants. It is paid once yearly near the end of Ramadan just before the 'Id al-Fitr.

Zamzam : the well in the Haram of Makka which has the best water in the world!

Allahumma salli ala sayyedina Muhammidan
abdika wa rasulika'n-nabiyyi'l-ummiyy
wa ala alihi wa sahbihi wa sallim

O Allah, bless our master Muhammad,
Your slave and Your Messenger, the unlettered Prophet,
and his family and his companions and grant them peace.

❂   ❂   ❂   ❂   ❂

By the same Author

The Last Prophet
may the blessings and peace of Allah be on him
and on his family and on his companions and followers

The Wives of the Prophet
Fatima az-Zahra
Asma bint Abi Bakr

The Journey of Ahmad and Layla

The Moghuls

The Difficult Journey
The Way Back

Dajjal, the AntiChrist
The Next World Order

Making History

As Co-Author with Muhammad Ata'ur-Rahim

Jesus, Prophet of Islam – *Revised Edition*

For Christ's Sake – *Part One* of the *Revised Edition*
of *Blood on the Cross*

Islam in Andalus – *Part Two* of the *Revised Edition*
of *Blood on the Cross*

As Co-Author with Abdal-Haqq and A'i'sha Bewley

The Islamic Will

✻   ✻   ✻   ✻   ✻

BIBLIOGRAPHY

Qur'an, from *Allah*. Translations by Muhammad Pickthall and by Muhammad Yusuf Ali and most recently and especially by Hajj Abdalhaqq and A'i'sha Bewley. Madinah Press. 1999.

A Dictionary and Glossary of the Qur'an, by John Penrice. Curzon Press. 1979.

A Glossary of Islamic Terms, by 'A'isha Bewley. Ta-Ha Publishers Ltd. 1998.

Al-Muwatta', of *Imam* Malik. Translated by 'A'isha 'Abdarahman at-Tarjumana and Ya'qub Johnson. Diwan Press. 1982.

Ar-Risala, of *Imam* Ibn Abi Zaid al-Qairwani. Translated by Alh. Bello Muhammad Daura. Northern Nigerian Publishing Co. Ltd. 1983.

Handbook on Islam, Iman, Ihsan, of *Shaykh* Uthman Dan Fodio. Translated by 'A'isha 'Abdar-Rahman Bewley. Diwan Press. 1978.

The Foundations of Islam, of *Qadi* 'Ayad. Translated by 'A'isha 'Abdarahman at-Tarjumana. Diwan al-Amir Publications. 1982.

Ash-Shifa', of *Qadi* 'Iyad. Translated by 'A'isha 'Abdarahman at-Tarjumana. Madinah Press. 1991.

Life of Muhammad, of Ibn Ishaq. Translated by Guillaume. Oxford University Press. 1978.

Life of Muhammad, by Martin Lings. Allen and Unwin. 1983.

The Life of Muhammad, by Tahia Al-Ismail. Ta-Ha Publishers Ltd. 1988.

Sahih, of *Imam* Bukhari. Translated by Dr. Muhammad Muhsin Khan. Crescent Publishing House. 1974.

Sahih, of *Imam* Muslim. Translated by 'Abdal-Hamid Siddiqui. Nusrat Ali Nasri for Kitab Bhavan. 1987.

Sunan, of *Imam* Abu Da'ud. Translated by Ahmad Hasan. Sh. Muhammad Ashraf. 1984.

The Gardens of the Righteous, of *Imam* Nawawi. Translated by Zafrullah Khan.

Mishkat al-Masabih. Translated by Professor Robson. 1972.

Forty Hadith, of *Imam* Nawawi. Translated by Ezedin Ibrahim and Denys Johnson-Davies. The Holy Qur'an Publishing House. 1976.

Forty Hadith Qudsi, from *Allah.* Translated by Ezzedin Ibrahim and Denys Johnson-Davies. The Holy Qur'an Publishing House. 1980.

The Book of Strangers, by Ian Dallas. Victor Gollancz. 1972.

The Way of Muhammad, by Shaykh 'Abd'al-Qadir as-Sufi. Diwan Press. 1974.

Root Islamic Education, by Shaykh 'Abd'al-Qadir al-Murabit. Diwan al-Amir Publications. 1982.

Diwans of the Darqawa. Translated by 'A'isha 'Abdarahman at-Tarjumana. Diwan Press 1980.

The Darqawi Way, of *Shaykh* Mawlay al-'Arabi ad-Darqawi. Translated by 'A'isha 'Abdarahman at-Tarjumana. Diwan Press. 1979.

The Meaning of Man, by *Shaykh* 'Ali al-Jamal. Translated by 'A'isha 'Abdarahman at-Tarjumana. Diwan Press. 1978.

The Basic Research, by *Shaykh* Ahmad ibn Muhammad ibn 'Ajiba. Translated by Abdalkhabir al-Munawwarah and Haj Abdassabur al-Ustadh and revised and edited by Shaykh Abdalqadir as-Sufi. Madinah Press. 1998.

Qur'anic Tawhid, by Shaykh 'Abd'al-Qadir as-Sufi. Diwan Press. 1981.

Indications from Signs, by Shaykh 'Abd'al-Qadir as-Sufi. Diwan Press. 1982.

Allahumma salli ala sayyedina Muhammidan
abdika wa rasulika'n-nabiyyi'l-ummiyy
wa ala alihi wa sahbihi wa sallim

O Allah, bless our master Muhammad,
Your slave and Your Messenger, the unlettered Prophet,
and his family and his companions and grant them peace.

The Life of Muhammad by Tahia Al-Ismail provides an accurate and concise historical account of the main events in the Prophet Muhammad's life, may Allah bless him and grant him peace.

Available from all good bookshops.

Published by: Ta-Ha Publishers Ltd.
                1 Wynne Road
                London SW9 0BB

❂   ❂   ❂   ❂   ❂

About the Author

Ahmad Thomson was born at Fort Jameson, in Northern Rhodesia – now known as Chipata, in Zambia. He began his schooling in Marandellas, in Southern Rhodesia – now known as Marondera, in Zimbabwe – boarding at Ruzawi and Peterhouse schools. In 1966 he went to Eastbourne College in England and then on to Exeter University where he was awarded an LL.B. (Hons.) in 1972. Although the author was given a Christian education, he stopped going to church as soon as it was no longer compulsory, and a year after leaving University, he embraced Islam at the hand of the Raja of Mahmudabad, *alehi rahma*, who was the Director of the Islamic Cultural Centre in London at that time, on the 13th of August 1973.

After keeping close company with his guide and teacher, Shaykh Abdal-Qadir al-Murabit, for three years – during which time he was co-author with Colonel Muhammad Ata'ur-Rahim of *Jesus, Prophet of Islam* and *Blood on the Cross* – and after going on the pilgrimage to Makka in 1977, the author recommenced his legal studies in 1978. After being awarded a Diploma in Law by the City University, London, he passed his Bar Examinations in 1979 and was called to the Bar on the 26th of July 1979 in Gray's Inn. After completing his pupillage as a barrister in 1980, the author travelled in the Middle and Far East before working on several books, including *Dajjal – The king who has no clothes*, *The Moghuls*, *The Journey of Ahmad and Layla*, *The Difficult Journey*, *The Way Back* and *The Next World Order*.

In 1991 the author resumed his career as a barrister, as well as writing books for younger readers, including *The Wives of the Prophet*, *Fatima az-Zahra* and *Asma bint Abi Bakr*. He recently completed the revised editions of the books which he first wrote with Colonel Rahim, *alehi rahma*: *Jesus, Prophet of Islam* – and *Blood on the Cross* now comprising two volumes entitled *For Christ's Sake* and *Islam in Andalus* – as well as a revised edition of his book on the Dajjal which is now entitled *Dajjal – the AntiChrist*. As well as completing *The Next World Order* the author has also written two further books entitled *Making History* and this book, *The Last Prophet*, may Allah bless him and grant him peace.